PRIZEFIGHTER

PRIZEFIGHTER

THE SEARING AUTOBIOGRAPHY OF BRITAIN'S
BAREKNUCKLE BOXING CHAMPION

DECCA HEGGIE

JOHN BLAKE

Published by John Blake Publishing Ltd,
3 Bramber Court, 2 Bramber Road,
London W14 9PB, England

www.johnblakebooks.com

www.facebook.com/johnblakebooks ▪
twitter.com/jblakebooks ▪

This edition published in 2017

ISBN: 978 1 78606 390 8

British Library Cataloguing-in-Publication Data:

A catalogue record for this book is available from the British Library.

Design by www.envydesign.co.uk

Printed in Great Britain by CPI Group (UK) Ltd

1 3 5 7 9 10 8 6 4 2

Papers used by John Blake Publishing are natural, recyclable products made from
wood grown in sustainable forests. The manufacturing processes conform to the
environmental regulations of the country of origin.

Every attempt has been made to contact the relevant copyright-holders,
but some were unobtainable. We would be grateful if the appropriate people
could contact us.

John Blake Publishing is an imprint of Bonnier Publishing
www.bonnierpublishing.com

To my parents, Derek and Barbara, for the love
and support you've always given me

CONTENTS

Preface		ix
Introduction		xi
Chapter One	BLACK EYES AND BLACK TIES	1
Chapter Two	INSPIRATION, EDUCATION AND CONFRONTATION	15
Chapter Three	HOME AND AWAY	29
Chapter Four	B–BAD TIMES	45
Chapter Five	LOVE AND OTHER DRUGS	63
Chapter Six	COPS AND BOTHER	79
Chapter Seven	OSCAR NIGHTS AND OTHER FIGHTS	95
Chapter Eight	SHAMROCK, SHENANIGANS AND A SAWN-OFF	107
Chapter Nine	TWICE THE PRICE	121
Chapter Ten	BLACK DOGS AND BLACK WIDOWS	133

Chapter Eleven   BATTLE OF THE BALES   149

Chapter Twelve   WHAT PRICE FAME?   163

Chapter Thirteen   OPPOSITION ALL THE WAY   179

Chapter Fourteen   LIGHTS, CAMERA, ACTION   193

Chapter Fifteen   BAD BLOOD AND BAD TIMING   209

Chapter Sixteen   FERTILE GROUND FOR A FIGHTER   221

Chapter Seventeen   THE GUV'NOR   235

Epilogue   255

PREFACE

'You can get a couple of years for beating the shit out of another bloke or a couple of grand. I chose to do the latter.'

I'm not one for looking back 'cause you can't change the past. The future is what I focus on because that is something I can shape but, in the writing of this book, I have been forced to revisit my past and it isn't pretty – at times it's been downright painful. It has also been cathartic. Talking about my life has made me realise how much the past has shaped the man I have become.

This is my story, in my own words, taken down and presented by my good friend and author, Stephen Wood, but not as a chronology; just in the order the stories came to me. That's how my head works and how I'd tell them to any of you if we were face to face.

I've told Stephen things I didn't think I would ever tell anyone – not even my family– but now I'm about to tell all of you. We'll delve into my past and the present in the only way I know how – honestly.

The future? I can't predict that but perhaps you'll be able to read about it in my next book. First though, let's deal with how I got to this point.

For the uninitiated, let me address one of the many misconceptions about my sport. Bareknuckle fighting is not an illegal activity provided it is licensed and takes place in a ring or between bales. Nor should it be confused with the 'anything-goes' brawls where biting and gouging, elbows and knees, and stamping and kicking are all part and parcel of the fight. In those sorts of tear-ups the combatants suffer terrible injuries; sometimes even die from their injuries. Barbaric stuff: those guys must be either utterly desperate for money or completely mental – probably both. Having said all that, I have taken part in three 'unsanctioned' bareknuckle bouts, which I will go into in greater detail later in the book.

The expression 'unlicensed fighting' refers to legally organised boxing matches not sanctioned by the British Boxing Board of Control but they are not the only sanctioning authority. What I do is sanctioned by the English Boxing Federation and lawful. That's not something I can say about everything I have done in my life.

INTRODUCTION

Depression – also known as The Black Dog. I don't know why. Maybe 'cause it's a sneaky bastard, which hides in the dark and bites when you least expect it. I think it's more like a stalker that lurks in the shadows of your subconscious. You know it's there but are never quite sure when it might strike. You're never alone with depression but – and here's the weird part – when it gets a grip of you, it really feels like you are totally (and I mean totally) isolated. Black Dog or stalker: either way, it's a bastard to live with and it will ultimately destroy you if you don't fight back.

I'll tell you when it can't strike: when you're toe-to-toe with some proper hard bastard intent on knocking seven bells out of you. Depression is a negative energy. In a bareknuckle fight there is no room for negativity. When you have to face the men I've fought, you have to believe you are invincible, 100 per cent, otherwise you've lost before the first punch is thrown.

In a taut, claustrophobic but electrically charged atmosphere of testosterone and adrenaline – body heat, body odour, alcohol and who knows what else – the crowd and assorted hangers-on are baying, yelling and cursing. It's all directed at two big lads in particular, both stripped to the waist, bloodied and bruised.

Most of the gobbing off is encouragement, each faction urging their man on; some of it abuse or the partisan appeals of gamblers who only care about the guy they've got money riding on – all of it punctuated by chanting.

"Deh-Kah, Deh-Kah – Mahhh-sheeeeen, Mahhh-sheeeen. "

I hear them but shut it all out. For me, be it in the ring or pit, concentration comes easy. In the thick of battle, it's nothing more than white noise. I have to focus on the job 'cause what is a dead cert is that the bloke I'm fighting has only me in his sights – and the purse on his mind. Every punch he lands is a wake-up call and the metallic tang of blood on my tongue, as it seeps from my lips and gums, is a reminder that he's getting through my defences, but I couldn't give a fuck.

I can soak up his bombs all day. The question is: Can he take mine? I've taken the best shots some of the hardest men on the bareknuckle circuit have ever thrown. Not only am I still standing but, having survived all they had in their impressive arsenals, I went on to beat them all.

This was no journeyman pro but a very hard and experienced brawler, with a punch like a steam-hammer. Suddenly, he switches his attack and dips and hooks under my elbow into my ribs. A liver-splitter intended to crease me and it's gonna hurt. Fuck me, and how, but he can have that shot on me 'cause, by letting him through, he drops his guard. Through gritted teeth I ignore the pain and deliver a vicious left cross over the top that slams into his temple. Nailed him! He staggers sideways but my right fist crashes into his cheek and checks him. Jelly-legged and dazed, he tries to back-pedal out of danger but he's going nowhere except down. I launch into a series of ferocious combinations, arms flailing like Bez Berry on a cocktail of Es an' whizz as he tries to fend off my onslaught, but his legs collide with the bales and he sits.

The ref jumps in unnecessarily; I've already stopped. I'm a gentleman fighter who never hits a man when he's down. The ref gets eye-to-eye with him. He's groggy but he's nodding as he steals the opportunity to suck some much needed air into his lungs. The plucky fucker isn't for throwing in the towel. He's brave, I'll give him that. With a growl, he barges past the ref and launches a last-ditch, all-or-nothing Exocet my way. Bez Berry has suddenly morphed into Rocky Balboa. If it connects, I'm in big trouble. It doesn't. The last punch he'll throw in this fight slides harmlessly past me and I take him out with a peach to the sweet spot on his exposed jaw.

Blood and drool splatter the front row of spectators as he tumbles sideways over the bales and skittles some of them. It's over. He went down fighting courageously. In this game, someone always does.

I'm undefeated in the bareknuckle discipline at the time of going to press and that's why I'm the champion. Nobody ever taught me how to fight but that's OK 'cause I never learned how to lose either. To be honest, I don't even like fighting. Maybe I do it to punish myself for all the grief I've put my family through. Or for betraying the one girl I have truly loved.

Despite being unbeaten, every one of those fights has been

a seriously hard-earned victory. It isn't just the winner that ends up licking his wounds in a bareknuckle bout, you know. Cracked bones, dislocated knuckles, split brow-ridges and lips, broken teeth and busted snouts are par for the course. Oh yeah, all in a day's work.

Let's not kid ourselves: you're putting your life on the line when you're up against the best in the game but those are the risks we take. I've taken on some deadly fighters, built like tower blocks with fists like wrecking balls. Honestly, a payday isn't the only thing at stake; danger comes with the job. Acknowledged, accepted, a tap of the fists and let's get the business done, boys.

Welcome to my world. My name's Decca Heggie and I'm The Guv'nor.

CHAPTER ONE

BLACK EYES AND BLACK TIES

Not all bareknuckle fighters are blunt instruments; grunting, seething lumps of muscle and calloused fists. Least ways, I'm not. But what we do is about as primal as being human in the twenty-first century gets. A bareknuckle bout is just that: a fist-fight without gloves. However, most of us have our hands bound with bandages but that's simply to prevent infection. *What?* The human mouth plays host to millions of harmful bacteria which, if they get into your bloodstream, can cause very serious – even life-threatening – infections. Really, ask your GP.

So what is it that draws men like me so readily into brutal confrontation? Good question. Cash is always a good incentive. We're just modern-day gladiators who pit their strength and power, martial skills and courage against another for prize money – and the entertainment of the crowd. Yes, there's a purse up for grabs but none of us do it for that alone.

Our motives go much deeper. Hopefully, by the end of this book you might uncover the answer to the question of why and, who knows, a few other mysteries surrounding this most ancient of sports.

Our sport, like boxing, is governed by certain rules: as a gentleman fighter I observe them to the letter. So that you get a true understanding of the sacrifices we make and what being a champion means, this account of my life sees no holds barred.

My name is Derek Heggie but you can call me Decca. I'm a professional bareknuckle fighter (not to be confused with a professional boxer). Mine is a pared down, stripped to the bone, most basic version of the noble art of fighting. It's the crude, pre-Marquis of Queensbury ancestor of modern-day boxing; the discarded blueprint, if you like, of the three minute-round, gloved martial art you are all more familiar with thanks to greats like Sugar Ray Robinson, Rocky Marciano, Mike Tyson and (the best ever, in my opinion) Mohammed Ali.

As of the 16 October 2016, I hold the honour of being known as The Guv'nor. A title that is not bestowed lightly but one that is earned through blood, sweat and pain in a ring. To win it I took on the holder of four British heavyweight boxing titles and five Commonwealth titles, Julius Francis. This man also fought for the European title twice and against four future world-heavyweight title holders and still some deny his credentials as a worthy opponent. Well, let me state for the record that they are talking bollocks.

Having told you that, let's get one thing clear right here and now: I am no Lenny McLean. He was an original, a one off, a rough, tough East End boy from Hoxton in London, whereas I'm a northerner, born and raised just a few miles from the Scottish border in the historic city of Carlisle. Two fighting men from opposing ends of our great country united by (a) my profound respect for his memory and achievements, (b) the brutal trade we both plied, and (c) that legendary title: The Guv'nor.

We do have something else in common, mind: Lenny was a right hard bastard and, like my dad before me, so am I.

I'm often asked how I got into this game. It might surprise you to know that fighting didn't come naturally to me, despite my dad's well-earned rep around Carlisle as a proper hard-case. It actually started when I was thirteen, after years of being bullied, but it must have been in my blood or my genes, lying dormant until my dad gave it a bit of a shake. By my late teens and twenties I was scrapping just for the hell of it, often as not when I was half-pissed or off my face on Charlie, or both. If you don't believe me, ask just about any bouncer in Carlisle that worked on the doors around the turn of the millennium. Drunk, wired on coke and with a point to prove, I was a doorman's worst nightmare, unless it was me looking after the door. That was different. I'd greet you with a smile.

Looking back, my life was a mess. Mum and Dad were pulling their hair out. Yeah, I was having fun – or at least I thought I was – but coke and booze can make you believe even the worst of times are a fuckin' blast, until you come back down and dry out. In truth, I was heading absolutely nowhere. Anyway, one day Dad gave me a tug – and when my dad clicks hold of you and gives you that look, trust me, you pay attention.

He said, 'If you don't cut all this shit out, son, the only place you're going is jail.' He was speaking from experience, having done time for breaking a lad's legs in reprisal after he got jumped by a gang and the shit kicked out of him. He battered the whole fuckin' lot of them, one after the other, but saved the worst punishment for their cowardly ring leader and got sent down for his trouble.

'But if you must fight,' he continued, 'if you really feel the need for a tear up now and again, I'll sort some out for you.'

I've got to tell you, I thought he was just taking the piss but no, he was serious and went on to explain, 'You could even earn a few quid out of it.'

So I'm thinking, '*Result!* Show me the money.' Bless him, my dad has always come through for his kids. So that's how I got into the fight game, on the bill at black-tie nights, which eventually led to bareknuckle fighting. You know the sort of thing: after-dinner entertainment for businessmen; a couple of eager (or is that ego-driven?) bruisers enjoying a good old ruck in the boxing ring. Those types of events are all above board and, licensed by the English Boxing Federation (EBF), the organisation that oversees The Guv'nor fight.

That was back in 2006 at The Hilltop Hotel, Carlisle. I fought a really tough bloke called Mickey German. I was overweight, unschooled, lacking in experience, technique and finesse but I met Mickey's far greater experience and skills with raw power and pure Heggie-born aggression, which saw me emerge triumphant.

The Machine had won on his debut. With the ref holding my arm aloft, the crowd's applause ringing in my ears and the purse in my arse pocket, I was hooked. Machine? Well, most people in the game adopt a handle and that's the one I chose. I was a huge fan of Ian 'The Machine' Freeman from Durham, the former World Heavyweight MMA Champion. I should have asked him really but, now that I'm a champion in my own right, I'm sure Ian won't mind.

The downside of these bouts saw me notch up my only ever losses – on points. *Points!* I wasn't in the ring to score fuckin' points. I went in there to knock the other fucker out but the first time it happened, and in subsequent fights when the other guy's glove was raised, it was because I couldn't nail the slippery bastards.

The trouble was that I had had no training or coaching and did little or no preparation for the fights. I just turned up, gloved up and got down to business. I had no background in boxing; hadn't even been inside a boxing gym until Macca started managing me. I was a coke-head and street-fighter who, often as not, was off his tits on the stuff by the time the bell went. What a muppet.

When I climbed into that ring, it was with the sole intention of a proper tear-up. Yet all the while, these more experienced boxers were picking me off with point-scoring little jabs and counters. It wasn't as if any of them hurt me, whereas I'm sure the clouts I managed to land always did. I never suffered a knockout – not even a standing count – but none of that mattered. I had been out-pointed and I lost. I don't mind telling you, it got under my skin losing in that fashion and so I looked around for the type of event that suited a street-fighter like me better.

Bareknuckle and pit-fighting glory beckoned. Knock-down or knockout punches, not 'points mean prizes' in that arena. Lucky for me then that, for a price, there are plenty of seriously tasty fighters out there who are only too happy to step up and get it on. Oh, and the occasional silly pretender. Anyway, ten ferociously contested bouts later I was crowned British Champion.

Not bad for an ex-glue sniffer from a Carlisle council estate who, until a short while ago, was lost in a fog of nose candy and heading for oblivion, eh?

Now I know that there will be some sceptics and detractors reading this book and saying, 'British Champion, my arse! He's never fought me, or what's-his-face, or thingamajig.' Fair shout but to all of them I say, 'For a start, I didn't invent the title and I won it fair and square but, hey, give me a chance. I've only been at this game for three years and in that time I've averaged over three fights a year. That's not bad going by any fighter's measure. So I will get around to you and you and you too *but* a word to the wise: be careful what you wish for.'

So what's my secret? Well, there's no silver bullet or magic formula. A number of things combine to mould a champion, especially from the sort of basic, raw material I had to go to work with when I first got into this game. For a start, I now have a proper switched-on and dedicated manager: Alan McDermott. A top-man is Macca, as he's better known around our town, and a good friend of many years' standing. Then there's my family and a broader, supportive team and network of totally reliable friends, all of them key to my success. But once I step into that ring or pit, be it gloved or bare fisted, the team can only watch – the outcome is all down to me.

So what do I bring to the party? Apart, that is, from hours of sheer hard graft pumping iron in the gym, lung-busting runs on the roads and tracks of the northern fells around Carlisle, or burning carbs off on the bike. Well, around seventeen and a half stone of raw power, give or take a pound or two, not to mention the furious sparring sessions, bag and pad work, as well as tractor-tyre flipping. Then throw natural aggression and street-fighting *nous* and combine all this with an above-average pain threshold and I'm good to go.

Once I discovered I could fight, I lost all fear of being hit. In fact, I get an adrenaline rush when the blows start to rain in, which I can only liken to a sexual experience. I don't mean that I get a hard-on, so put that image out of your mind – I'm there to cream my opponent, not ream him.

The best way I can describe the level of excitement I experience and how I react to what is happening is that for every action there is a reaction. And that's about as much as I can remember from school science classes. The more they pour it on, the more they fuel my lust for victory. Punches and pain fire me up; they energise me and, the harder they hit me, the greater the buzz I get, which is a big problem for the gadgey I'm fighting. Gadgey? Oh, that's Carlisle craic for guy, fella, bloke – geezer, if you like.

That 'Black Dog' has followed me about all my life – I think I first felt it snapping at my heels during a particularly difficult time in my childhood and, no, I'm not going to regale you with tales of child abuse – at least not at the hands of my parents.

Long before all the fighting and the drug abuse I was just another ordinary kid growing up in Old Harraby, a council estate on the outskirts of Carlisle. I happened to be blessed with a wonderful mum and dad, Barbara and Derek Snr. They did a great job of raising their kids: me, my kid brother Barry and my sister Cassandra (Cassie). Nowadays, my parents lavish the same degree of love and devotion on their beautiful grandchildren.

In a book whose spine is practically breaking with the

weight of hard bastards contained between the front and back cover, here's the first name you should take note of and remember: Derek 'Decca' Heggie Snr – my dad. I swear down that, in his prime, he was a lot harder than I am but he was never a bully. He cannot abide bullies and I've inherited that same intolerant gene.

From about the age of eight, up until I was thirteen, I was the victim of constant bullying from a group of lads around our neighbourhood. The worst of them was a kid called Jamie; he would batter me just about every time our paths crossed. I can't remember ever doing a thing to provoke him; in fact, I went out of my way not to give him the slightest excuse. All the kids around our estate acknowledged Jamie as the local hard-case but that wasn't good enough for that nasty twat. He knew he had power over us and he revelled in it. Nothing gave him greater pleasure than to walk into the disco at the community centre and smack me around in front of everyone for nothing, then just swagger back out, laughing often as not.

At moments like that I just wanted to die. I hated him for making me feel so pathetic, for making me look such a useless wimp, for not fighting back, for not being more like my dad. If I'd really thought about it, I wasn't the coward, Jamie was; all bullies are and the very worst are sadists. You will have all known or encountered one or more in your lifetime, I'm sure. Now take a moment and think of their victim(s). Were they always weaker? Of course they were. Was the bully you're thinking of in any danger from their victim? No, none whatsoever. Did the bully encourage others to join in? Often as not, especially if they secretly felt they needed help to achieve their objective. These are the choices bullies and cowards make. Pick on the weak, target the vulnerable, and the pleasure they get from doing that, from hurting or humiliating someone else, is nothing but pure sadism.

It took me a while to realise it but Jamie's tough exterior was just that; a shell he hid behind; nothing but front with fuck all to back it up when push came to shove. Looking back, I can't ever remember him taking on another kid that had any kind of rep to match or better the one he had cultivated by beating up smaller, weaker kids. Whereas I can honestly say, hand on heart, I've never taken on a rival who wasn't capable of doing me real damage – or at least acted the part and made all the right noises until I called his bluff and knocked him spark out.

Today, despite the reputation I have earned and the respect I am shown in most quarters, which gives me power over a lot of men, I never wield it without very good reason. Hand on heart, I would much rather make a friend of anyone than light that spark of enmity. So don't be shy: if we meet, offer your hand in friendship. I promise you this: I will reciprocate. As a man, Jamie has never summoned up the courage to offer his hand and apologise for terrorising me through those formative years and, to be honest, I'm not sure I'd accept. The painful memories run far too deep.

Even when he wasn't dishing out a hiding, Jamie would intimidate and scare the shit out of me, just for a laugh. Knowing how scared I was of him was all part of the fun for that horrible bastard. He loved it. Sometimes there would be a few of them with him giving the orders and delivering the occasional sly dig into my ribs or face. On other occasions, when he wasn't around, his gang would jump me and do the job for him. Then they'd track their leader down, bragging and kissing his arse. I can hear them now:

'Hey, Jamie, guess who we've just fuckin' battered? Yeah, Derek Heggie.'

Yeah, all good fun, eh, boys? But who's laughing now? Many of those lads still live in and around the Harraby area or I see them knocking about the city and, like the cowardly twats they always were, they crap themselves when they clock me coming along. I've actually seen some of the spineless bastards duck off down the nearest side street or into a shop. Not being a bully, I would never lay a finger on them these days. The look I give them is enough. Still, it does make me smile to see the look on their faces. They can be sure I will never forget them or their cruelty and, from hereon in, they will skulk by in my shadow and always remain there – in the shadow of a champion.

Down the generations, there has been a tradition among squabbling kids of threatening one another with their dads but I can honestly say that I never did that. I was too embarrassed to ever tell my dad that I was being bullied. Knowing what a hard bastard he was, and aware of his fearsome reputation, I always thought he'd be either mortified or furious with me for being so weak and cowardly but I should have trusted him. I should have trusted in his love for his children and his instincts when it came to fighting his corner or when dealing with other tough guys, wannabes and bullies. Had I done so, I might have saved myself years or torment. My dad never steps aside for anyone but plenty of men avoid him, or have learned to do so the hard way if they ever made the mistake of taking him on.

The most significant moment came one day when I walked through the door sporting a shiner, after yet another battering from Jamie. Dad wanted to know who'd given it to me. I was too frightened to tell him at first, knowing what he would do. No, not go and clip the little bastard. That's not dad's way. He'll back you all the way but he won't fight your fights for you. But Dad wasn't gonna have that, so I reluctantly told him about Jamie and his mates.

Time seemed to stand still and that all too familiar look came over his grizzled face; the one that says, 'Did he now? Thinks he's a tough guy, does he? Well, we'll just fuckin' see about that.' Minutes later I was being frogmarched around to Jamie's house. Dad banged on the door and told Jamie's old lad to get his boy out on the front toget this sorted; a one-to-one fight: me versus Jamie. Of course, Jamie's dad wasn't going to argue with the notorious Decca Heggie – not he if wanted his snout to stay the shape it was when he'd opened the door. Duly, he presented my nemesis.

To be honest, I was terrified but Dad looked me in the eye and told me I could beat him. In fact, Dad knew I could but I just didn't believe in myself. As we stepped up, encouraged quietly but firmly by our respective dads, for the first time ever, I saw fear in that miserable bully's eyes but I saw the same look in his dad's eyes and put it down to my dad being there. You have to understand that my dad was renowned and feared not only in Old Harraby but all over Carlisle. He had a reputation not only as a hard-case but for being a bit of a fuckin' maniac.

Even with Dad there though – and to his total embarrassment – I bottled it and wouldn't fight Jamie. Dad pushed me out of the gate and Jamie went back inside. I was led home with Dad muttering his disappointment all the way. Then, behind the door, he rattled my arse just once with a slipper. Punished for my cowardice. No one reading this should condemn him for that. I didn't then and I still don't. He is a proud, hard man from a proud, hard background and his eldest boy had wimped out. Shame heaped upon shame. The thing is that the fear I saw in Jamie's eyes was the fear of being confronted on an equal basis. I just didn't recognise it at the time. Add to that the fact that the man behind me was more than a match for his father. The bully had been confronted and shown a hint of his true colours but, once again, his victim proved weaker.

Feeling sorry for myself and for my dad, I waited for him to go out and snatched his Lenny McLean video from his stash of VHS tapes and stuck it in the player. One day I would show my dad that I was made of the same stuff. One day I would fight. One day Jamie would fall and fall hard, just like Lenny's opponents.

That horrible sensation of crippling fear, of shame and embarrassment at my own weakness, of being alone, frightened and friendless, has never left me. Yes, I still get frightened. If you had to face the men I fight, you'd be frightened too. If not, you are either as mad and bad as Charlie Bronson or too stupid to be frightened. You can hide from bullies but not from the fear of them. Just as I learned to overcome my terror, I have developed a mechanism for harnessing the energy fear can generate. Instead of hiding or running away, I don't just stand and fight – I launch into an all-out attack.

That frightened little pup they teased and tormented, thumped and kicked, humiliated and ridiculed for all those years eventually turned – and he turned big-style. My feeble whimpering became a ferocious snarl and a lone wolf emerged, but no ordinary wolf – the daddy of them all, an Alpha male and one that is now capable of taking on and tearing apart Jamie and his whole pack of arse-lickers at the same time.

Talking about those dark days of my childhood and my dad's intervention brings me neatly around to him. The first thing I want to do is apologise to him, personally, before all of you as witnesses reading this book.

Some time ago I was managed by a man that goes by the name of Joe B-Bad (Joe Smith-Brown) – another name to remember but not necessarily for the right reasons. I'll tell you more of him later. For a while Joe and I became very close. Then one day I got into a row with my dad and, in the heat of the moment, I told him that Joe would be a better father to me than he had ever been.

That was a lie. Worse than that, it was malicious 'cause I knew it was the only way I could hurt him. Yes, I could have stuck one on him but, make no mistake, he'd have torn right back into me. To this day, I have a sufficiently healthy respect for that old scrapper to avoid ever getting into gear with him. Age has not diminished his pluck or fighting prowess.

Not only was it a spiteful thing to say, it was totally uncalled for because I knew then, just as I know now, that I have the best father any man could ask for; even when he is rowing with me or giving me a hard time, he's doing it because he cares, because he loves me. It took a while to figure that out and, now that I'm older and a little bit wiser (but not much), I realise that, by always being honest with me, Dad keeps me grounded; keeps me right.

I don't always agree with him but what I do know and will always be grateful for is that he is strong enough in his love for his kids to always do and say what he thinks is right, regardless of how we might react. I love my mum to the very depths of my soul and, although Dad and I never talk about such stuff, I love him just as much. I have more respect for him than any man I have ever met or will ever meet. Because of you, Dad, your son is a fighter and champion at that. Thank you – may I never cause you any shame or pain again.

OK, that's it: soppy stuff over with, for now. Ding, ding, seconds out...

CHAPTER TWO

INSPIRATION, EDUCATION AND CONFRONTATION

During the period when I was being constantly bullied by Jamie and his gang, I would wait until Mum and Dad were out or were asleep and sneak downstairs to borrow Dad's video of Lenny McLean's fights. Dad would never let us watch stuff like that because Lenny could, and often did, go right over the top in a fight. In that particular video, not only does he batter Mad Gypsy Bradshaw until he's flat-out on the canvas but then he barges the ref out of the way and stamps on Bradshaw's ribs and head.

It's funny but, whenever Dad was in the corner where he kept his VHS tapes, he would always notice that somebody had been messing with them. I'd play the innocent and bugger off out before I was betrayed by my blushes.

Regardless of the violence on display, watching McLean destroy his opponents somehow brought me comfort. At a deeper level, it became a source of inspiration. Although I had

15

no idea how I would make the transition from timid kid to fighting champion, the seed must have been sown.

Sometimes Lenny would annihilate an opponent in seconds but that wasn't what made the greatest impression on me. It was the raw aggression that ran through his veins and then exploded through his fists. I would daydream that one day I might be like that; unafraid of anyone and willing to take on all comers.

Motivational trainers tell us that, in order to achieve your goal, you must first believe that you can reach it and then visualise yourself succeeding. I think they call it positive affirmation. I used to watch those YouTube clips and picture myself in that ring smashing my opponents to pieces. Usually, my opponents would look uncannily like Jamie or one of his crew but the outcome was always the same: I would pulverise the bastards. Deep down, at some subconscious level, I guess I made that positive affirmation because today I hold that belt and title.

However, the game-changing showdown with Jamie had yet to happen and the likelihood of such a transformation seemed nothing more than an utter fantasy. Little did I realise, though, that I was only days away from settling that overdue score; that I would consign those aching fears to history. Consequently, as I watched my hero rampage around the ring laying waste to really tasty rivals, the victim mentality remained deeply embedded in me and continued to suppress the fighter within.

My rivals' teasing, tormenting and bullying had left me mentally scarred and still affects me to this day. Those painful memories are a powerful motivating factor but Jamie will get no thanks or credit for my success from me on that score. I'd much sooner we'd all grown up friends and that none of it had ever happen. We didn't and my life took an altogether different course.

Funny, isn't it, how some people go through life getting a kick out of causing pain, upsetting folk or from making enemies, while others gain far greater pleasure from making friends or bringing comfort to someone in need? Give me friendship any day. Many of the guys I have fought have become good friends. That might sound hard to believe but it is absolutely true. We test each other to the limit in combat but invariably hug, pat one another on the back and shake hands when the fight is over. That's what true fighters do; what genuine hard-men do.

Bullies skulk away feeling sorry for themselves when they've lost, with no thought whatsoever to what they have put their victims through before receiving their much-deserved comeuppance.

Be it pit or ring, bare knuckles or gloves, I don't care. Put enough money in the purse and a willing opponent in front of me and you've got yourself a fight. I've been asked if I'm the hardest man in Britain. Short answer: no. I'm not even the hardest man in my family. My dad was harder than me at my age but he was too busy providing for us all to get into this game. It probably never even crossed his mind to fight another gadgey for money. Then there's my cousin, Johnny Heggie. I reckon he's tougher than me. A proper hard-case, our Johnny, but, like my dad, a family man and a gentleman.

Mind you, Dad had his moments when he was younger. Now him I could write a book about. Our Johnny, though, he wouldn't bother anybody who didn't bother him or his own. So if you take my advice, don't bother him. I've never claimed to be the hardest man in Britain, nor will you ever hear me making such a claim but am I the hardest bareknuckle fighter? That's a bit of a daft question too. Based on the quality of the men I've beaten, the titles I hold and my standing in the rankings, I think I've earned the right to say yeah, I've got to be up there – *but!* Every unlicensed bareknuckle or pit fighter out there is an unknown quantity until you take him on. There are a lot I haven't fought and probably not enough years of fighting left in me to get around to them all.

There are the countless, anonymous men who rarely – maybe even never – get into fights; maybe go out of their way to avoid them. Truth be told, though, they would have all the tools to take anyone out if they tried. For every recognised master of any art, sport or discipline you care to mention out there in the big wide world there are undiscovered geniuses – ordinary people who will never realise their true potential; talented people destined to spend their lives in quiet obscurity and probably perfectly happy to do just that. Look around you. How many handy-looking lads pass you by in the street every day?

I say handy-looking but, to be honest, they don't even have to look the part. There's an old saying: 'Beware the quiet man.' And it's true. Our Johnny is a very good example of such people: quiet and unassuming but deadly in a scrap. Many a so-called hard-case has come unstuck when crossing the path of a complete stranger who refuses to back down. He promptly does the business before disappearing to continue his anonymous life. We've all heard such tales. How much untapped fighting talent must be out there?

So whether I'm the hardest is not for me to say or for anyone else to claim on my behalf. I've been the UK bareknuckle champion and UK pit-fighting champion – decide for yourself. What I can tell you for sure is this: the blokes I've fought are all hard men and, in their company, a pretender is soon found out. There is no margin for error and that's why I work so hard and prepare so rigorously now leading up to a fight.

The golden rules:

- Turn up ready and willing, conditioned and confident.
- Cut out the errors and exploit my opponent's.
- Expose any weaknesses I detect as we're slugging it out.
- Expect no quarter and give none.
- It stops when he drops or throws in the towel.

When I think about it, my golden rules applied during my school days. Not as a fighter at that time but as a footballer. North Cumbria Technology College was the secondary school I was sent to in 1995. Despite being a chubby kid – another source of unwelcome jibes and teasing – I was quite a naturally gifted footballer. Not a bad thing to excel at when you start at a new school and want to make a good impression and win over new friends.

There were some funny looks when 'Fatso' Heggie was selected for the school team but I soon proved worthy of my place. I progressed and got fitter and I went on to represent the county as well as the school. In my first year, though, I had also started playing for Arroyo under-twelves, as a defender. Although I lacked a classic footballer's build, being bigger than average for my age and more nimble than my size would otherwise suggest, I proved effective in defence.

Another kid, who became a good mate at that time, was

Gary Brown. He was our sweeper – as far as I'm concerned, one of the best defenders and readers of the game I ever played alongside. I was good but Gary was truly gifted. We only had a couple of decent individual players. I just mentioned two of them but Arroyo weren't a very good team. We notched up some totally embarrassing losses (8–0 and 6–0 wasn't unheard of on our scoresheet) so maybe I wasn't as effective in defence as memory serves but those regular drubbings tended to bring out the worst in me.

It might come as a surprise to you but I was prone to roughing up the opposition a bit. On reflection, my latent aggression reared its ugly head on the football pitch long before my dad dug it out in Jamie's front garden. In part, and I suppose, under controlled conditions, it was a safe environment in which I was able to offload some of the frustration I felt as a result of the endless bullying and name-calling I had suffered for so long. What was the worst that could happen? I might get sent off. Big deal: I could live with that.

Arroyo's manager was a fella called Eddie Jardine–a really good and dedicated bloke. Eddie was a well-known, respected figure back then on the youth-football circuit, not least for his commitment. Poor bugger, his team (our team) was a bit of a joke. To some extent, he encouraged my aggression on the field and applauded the way I used to scythe through players, taking man and ball. Maybe it did something to alleviate his disappointment as he watched us go down for yet another thumping but not before I'd sent half the opposition hobbling off the pitch, black and blue.

Even then, with his team regularly vying for bottom place in the league, Eddie put mine and Gary's futures ahead of Arroyo's success. He was forever pointing out to scouts and the managers of better teams what an asset his two best players would be to them. He really believed in us and saw prospects ahead, provided we played regularly alongside better players than his team attracted. Sure enough, Gary and I eventually moved on to play at a much higher level.

My confidence and aggressive behaviour on the football pitch was in sharp contrast, though, to how I conducted myself at school during my first couple of years. I was very quiet compared to most. The bullying had got to me. The last thing I wanted to do was attract the attention of other nasty lads. Slowly but surely, however, the Heggie gene that ran through my blood began to come to the fore. I became a bit of a nuisance, by just fooling around mostly. You know, cheek and similar disruptive behaviour in an attempt to make the other kids laugh 'cause, when you're considered a good laugh, kids tend to like you and, if they like you, they don't pick on you.

Being students at a so-called technology college, the staff regularly prodded us about future careers. Let's not kid ourselves: schools like mine were conceived to produce lower-level workers and artisans. Every so often a brainy bugger would emerge from our ranks and go on to university. The future they had mapped out for the rest of us was not what I had in mind at all. I used to tell them that I wanted to be a bodyguard. Naturally, that got a few laughs from classmates and teachers alike but I was absolutely serious. Once my fighting days are over, I still wouldn't mind exploring that possibility.

So if any mega-rich, global superstars are reading this, take note. If you want a proven hard-man looking after your arse, who will not step aside, regardless of whatever is coming your way, Decca Heggie will soon be available for hire – for a reasonable fee plus expenses, of course.

My favourite teacher was Mr Feeney. He taught one of my least favourite subjects: Maths. Shit, I still need a dictionary to spell Pythagoras. As for his fuckin' theorem, and despite Mr Feeney's best efforts, I still couldn't begin to explain its meaning or point. 'The square on the wotsit is equal to the sum of the what?' Even if it had made any sense to me, what possible use was it to a kid from Old Harraby? I can't say I've ever been bang into triangles. Threesomes, now you're talking – just joking – but pointy things with three sides? Err – nah, what's that about?

He was OK, was Mr Feeney. Firm, mind but, because he was also very fair, we got along really well. You knew where you were in his classroom. To this day, I much prefer to know where I stand with folk. Black and white, yes or no, whichever Mr Feeney said, that's what he meant. Kids need boundaries but they also need trust and it has to run both ways. We trusted him and he got the best out of us. That's because we knew where we stood and could have a laugh with him.

Trust engenders respect and, when a teacher enjoys the respect of his students and shows respect for them, it's a win-win scenario. That's what he did, ever so subtly and without ever giving us the impression that he wasn't in charge or in complete control of the situation. We even got away with swearing some of the time, dependent upon his mood. Never the 'C' word mind. Mr Feeney was pretty cool but drew the line at 'c**t'. Y'see, out of respect for him, even now, I've starred it out. Yeah, he was sound, was Mr Feeney, whereas some of the other teachers *were* c**ts!

There is something else I'd better make clear early on because I know this book will be read by some very impressionable people who will be thinking, 'If a fat little wimp from Carlisle can become the EBF and bareknuckle champion, I'm already halfway there 'cause I'm not fat and I'm not a wimp.'

Good for you. But – and it's a big BUT – for every Lennox Lewis, Rory McIlroy, Jessica Ennis-Hill, Lewis Hamilton and Andy Murray that rises to the top of their individual sport there are tens of thousands of really talented nearly-men and women. Many don't even make the starting gate. The reason those champion sportsmen and women became the best is that they had that indefinable extra something beyond self-belief, self-discipline, dedication and endless training and preparation routines.

The same goes in the bareknuckle business. What you have to ask yourself is this: 'Have I got that extra something?' If the answer is no or you're not quite sure, believe me, bareknuckle fighting is not the place to find out. Getting your brain rattled around your skull and facial features rearranged by a bloke with knuckles like granite cobbles is the hard way to find out that you've maybe over-estimated your pugilistic prowess.

Whatever *IT* is, I must have it because I have put away some of the best guys in the game. I mean them no disrespect. On the contrary, it takes a big man to step into that ring or square. It takes an even a bigger man to shake your hand after the kind of hammering we dish out. It takes a giant to come back for more. That's why I respect my opponents and especially the ones I've fought and beaten more than once. I respect any man who takes me on because they're gonna get hurt and they're under no illusions about that. Yet there they are, front and centre, stripped to the waist, fists raised and ready to rock.

That's not the only reason I show respect. It's also because I know that, just like me, they think they're invincible. Even if you're struggling to respect the man because you know him to be a proper horrible bastard, you've got to be wary of that mind-set or you'll soon come unstuck and end up taking a vicious hiding for nothing. One purse – winner takes all.

I can hear some of you asking, 'What about all those really hard gypsy fighters?' OK, let's deal with that thorny issue. No disrespect to them either but they don't fight on the same licensed circuit I operate in *and* their fighting tradition is a cultural thing as much as it is a sport. Yes, they fight for money but they also fight for the honour of their clan. They fight to settle debts, to settle bets and disputes, while other travellers bet on the outcome of *that* fight, which invariably begets another – and another, *ad infinitum*. They fight to settle feuds, half of which started with a bleedin' bareknuckle fight, for Christ's sake! It's a vicious circle; round and round they go. Nobody knows how it started. Nobody is willing to call an end to it for fear of losing face.

So no I haven't – and probably never will – fight a gypsy challenger. The main reason I won't (putting licensing and legal arguments aside) is that they're not very good losers. By that, I don't necessarily mean their individual fighters are bad losers. I'm sure many of them are true gentlemen and classy, straight-up, honest-to-goodness pugilists. It's their families – the wider clan – you've got to watch out for. Losing a fight, for some of them, is to lose face with *all* of them: the travelling community is a very proud people, as anyone who spends any time around them will attest.

Up at Hadrian's Camp to the north of Carlisle and out at Low Harker there are long-established resident communities of travellers and Cumbria has historically attracted those who choose to live on the move. Not only that, Cumbria also plays host to the largest gathering of gypsies and travellers in Britain at the annual Appleby Horse Fair. Needless to say, as a result, I regularly encounter travellers and quite often receive challenges. For all the reasons I have previously cited, I always politely decline.

They can read into that whatever they like and they do. I have my reasons and a professional strategy that places me on a different trajectory to their champions and long-established fighting tradition. In any case, why would I want to get bogged down in any of their ongoing dramas or get drawn into endless tit-for-tat disputes? Trust me: if they aren't satisfied with the outcome of a fistfight, it rarely ends with the shake of a hand. What am I saying? It never ends! Anyway, I'm pretty sure I'd get a tug from the EBF and a few harsh words in my lug if I let them bait me into taking one of them on.

Add to that all the money that will have been won and lost in bets and side bets. We're talking tens of thousands of pounds changing hands because they are generally betting men; I mean seriously high-stakes gamblers. Those kinds of losses bring out the very worst in some people and, in their world, the very worst is about as bad as it gets. Who wants to get caught up in all of that? I don't care how hard you think you are, you do not want a bunch of pissed-off pikeys banging at your door looking to settle a score, do you? Nah, me neither!

By the time I was fourteen, the bullying had finally stopped. Then, into my fifteenth year, I was walking down the street, heading home from the football field, when I met Jamie coming the other way. He stopped and barred my way with that by now familiar cocky sneer on his chops. Next thing you know, he started poking me in my chest and giving me all his old patter. I stood there for a moment thinking, 'Really? Are you seriously still into this sort of bollocks? Have we not moved on?' Apparently not. Or should I say, I had but he had reverted to type: hideous bully boy. What could I say? Nothing, it seemed; instead I let my fist do the talking. *Boom!* I whacked the cocky twat with an absolute peach of a shot. Wow! He went down like the sack of shit he was. I was no less stunned. Where the hell had that come from?

Six years of fear and tears, pain and humiliation suddenly exploded and I thought to myself, 'You're fuckin' dead, pal.' I don't know about the old 'Red Mist' coming down; I was more like raging hurricane. I just snarled like a wild dog and stamped all over the horrible c**t, just like Lenny did when Mad Gypsy Bradshaw nutted him as they touched gloves. It was the only time in my life that I have used my feet on a fallen opponent. I wasn't sorry at the time and I'm still unapologetic because that bullying arsehole deserved every kick and blow, just like Bradshaw did when he took liberties with Lenny.

Jamie finally got his just desserts in the winter of 1998. That was the year a fighting man was born – a future Guv'nor, even if I didn't know it then. I left him lying where he fell, battered, bruised, bloodied and blanked right out. It was to be our final violent encounter.

When I got home and told my dad that I'd sparked Jamie out, he didn't say much at first but I could tell that I'd restored the faith he'd shown in me that time in Jamie's front garden and I'd done it without his support; without the confidence I might have gained from having him in my corner. Eventually, Dad sat me down and said, 'Son, that's what to do. If they've got some imaginary problem with you, give 'em a real one. Fuck them over before they do you and ask questions afterwards if you're interested.' Of course, I couldn't ask Jamie what the fuck all that aggravation with me had been about – he wasn't conscious! Dad also advised that I never leave myself open for a sucker-punch. Be the one who walks away, not crawls or gets carried. It's advice I have always heeded. From thereon in, I've met any hassle head on. My wily street-fighter of a father instilled in his son the rules of street-fighting survival and a self-belief that has never deserted me.

With Jamie well and truly sorted, the rest of his crew had it coming. It was a proper buzz seeing them run from me after all those years as, in the space of a few short weeks, I tracked them all down. One by one, I filled them all in and it felt abso-fuckin'-lutely brilliant. The only problem I had then was that I'd started to enjoy it and a tear-up became something I did for fun.

'Get stuck in the minute it starts to look iffy.' That's what Dad had said and that's what I did. The same holds true in a pit fight. The moment the bell sounds or the ref says the fight is on, take the pain, stay on your feet and get the business done. Respect for your opponent is all well and good but not so much that you surrender any advantage.

CHAPTER THREE

HOME
AND AWAY

Carlisle folk aren't like any I've met anywhere else in Britain. We're proper stubborn bastards with flint under our skin and fire in our blood. We're borderers; a people who live in a city and region that has been fought over by the Scots and English since the Romans gave up trying to tame us and fucked off. The Ancient Britons didn't tend to keep written records, you see. The Picts that we constantly fought with back then, and who gave the Romans so much aggravation, didn't have a written language at all.

Take me: I'm English but Heggie is a Scottish name. My grandfather was a 'Sweaty' who migrated south looking for work but we Old Harraby Heggies don't think of ourselves as Jocks at all. That said, Carlisle has been part of the ancient Kingdom of Alba on a few occasions in the past, so who's to say that the rest of my lineage isn't Scottish? For hundreds of years the Scottish/English border ebbed and flowed, north and south. It was known as The Middle Lands and ever present throughout those long, turbulent and bloody years was the city of Carlisle.

We shared a common dialect and traditions back then and that messes with the heads of us border-city folk. We're not Scottish, yet many of us have roots on both sides of the border. We live beside and among Scots and, let's face it, are a hell of a lot closer to their capital than our own but we're English – if only just and northerners to our core.

People who live on a border always feel like outsiders; like they're on their own. Ask the Jocks in the Scottish Borders if you don't believe me. They aren't like those in the Central Belt or Highlands. They're more like us: bolshie, wary buggers, on their guard – and why? Because they're borderers and borderers never quite know who to trust. You hear the SNP banging on about their distrust of Westminster and how unfair it is that a place so far removed from Scotland holds sway over them. Just wander yourself up to Dumfries or Newcastleton or any other town just over the border and ask them if they trust their politicians in Edinburgh. Nuff said.

This is the frontier, the very northern fringe of England, and it butts right up against our southern Scottish neighbours. So it's hardly any wonder we Charvers (as we're known locally) developed a bit of a belligerent attitude. If you doubt me, pay a visit some time. Don't worry, you'll get a warm welcome and enjoy your stay. Make sure you check out the city's iconic castle. That massive, impregnable redoubt alone will tell you everything you need to know about Carlisle folks' attitude. 'This is our city, our home, and we don't yield to anyone.

Here's an interesting fact. Robert the Bruce, that great Scottish hero, was a borderer and Carlisle Castle was the family seat for a while. I'll tell you something else for a fact. He wasn't all that Scottish either. He was a nobleman of Norman stock who spoke Norman French, not the canny 'Clan Laird-cum-King' of Scottish myth and legend he's often portrayed as. All the same, he did the business for his adopted people and is rightfully revered north of the border.

Carlisle Castle's prominent position and formidable sandstone walls still seems to yell defiantly, 'Bring it on! ' – and many an army has – but our proud boast is this: Carlisle is the most besieged castle in England but one of few in the whole of the country never to have been taken by force. Maybe I should have called myself The Castle instead of The Machine, eh? Another of our little idiosyncrasies, as you'll discover when you visit, is that in Carlisle we often end a sentence with 'eh'. So what are you waiting for? An invitation?

Having laid the ghosts of bullying to rest and now brimming with confidence, naturally, I had also moved up into the under-fourteens football league but, being leaner and much fitter, as a striker for another team and under a new manager: my dad. Our team changed its name several times but, for ease, I'll call it Harraby Catholic Club and we had some great players. Gary Brown had followed me there and we found ourselves playing alongside lads like Craig Wilkinson, Paul Fiddler (aka Tid) and Stephen 'Archie' Archibald, who was my strike partner.

Archie was the best striker I ever took to the field with. He was the best goal poacher in the Cumbria under-fourteens league and, between us, we scored 153 goals in just 28 games. My tally was ninety-eight and Archie's fifty-five and that was just us two. Lads like winger Stuart Moffat – a great player, Stu, and, like me, a Harraby kid through and through – knocked a few in, as did Andy Tinning. Andy was, and still is, one of my best friends. Right through school to the present, we've been mates; even though we don't see each other as often as we used to, it's like we've never been apart when we do get together.

Andy has a family of his own now but, as a kid, I used to sleepover at his house. We'd amuse ourselves by drawing football stadia – I know, fuckin' football grounds. How totally nerdy is that? But that's how obsessed we were with the beautiful game. Andy's mam, Sandra, was a lovely woman, who was very close to my parents but sadly passed away after losing her long battle with alcoholism.

As under-fourteens, we went all season undefeated and won the league and the Cumberland County Cup. We were the best team in Cumbria and, through both under-fourteens seasons, we came top of the league. When we moved up into the sixteens age group, none of us was actually sixteen. We found ourselves playing against much older, more experienced lads and yet we still ended the season at the top of the league.

By that time, though, I had started going clubbing and thought of myself as a bit of a Jack-the-lad. I was regularly getting pissed up at the Freedom night club in Carlisle. They held 'all you can drink' nights for £9.99. Imagine that. A fifteen-year-old with enough money to pay the admission fee and a tenner left over could get absolutely battered – and I did.

On one such night, I was out with my mate Shaun Kenney. Shaun's a cracking lad and has been a good mate for years – a handy lad too; big and powerful. We were walking home from a night out having blown everything on booze when we got into a row with a group of lads. I can't remember what sparked it but it turned into a bit of a ruck. I ended up knocking three of them out and gave it no more thought. I was so trolleyed that I don't even remember if Shaun joined in. Knowing him, he will have done and probably dealt with the others because I do remember there were more than the three I took out.

Anyway, having sorted those clowns out, we continued on our way but they came after us. This time they had reinforcements in tow: a much older, much bigger and much harder bloke. Now remember, I was only a boy of fifteen but this fella was a grown man. The big bastard knocked me to the ground and then stamped on my head. What sort of a man does that to a kid? I'd maybe deserved a hiding – as I said, I can't remember who or what kicked off the original scrap – but he went right over the top. What I didn't do was put my feet into any of them or stamp on the arseholes when they were down. I tell you what: it's a good job my old lad didn't see him or he'd have ripped his spine out through the top of his head and reinserted it up his arse.

I was young and daft, full of life and steaming drunk but, hey, I took out three of them on my own before they called their match-winning sub onto the field. He scored with his first shot; put me on my arse and in the hospital for the night. It got proper ugly when my dad arrived. He was absolutely raging and went round A&E offering them all out but it wasn't any of them that had put me in there. A couple of the lads I had battered were in getting treatment too, you see and, quite naturally, their families had turned up as well.

Of course, the fella that had stomped me into the ground was nowhere to be seen. He probably thought the bizzies would turn up and lift him but he needn't have worried. We Heggies lick our own wounds, settle our own scores and don't ever grass. Had he been cocky enough to tag along, he would have ended up in intensive care. I swear I have rarely seen my old lad so fuckin' angry. With the mood he was in, he'd have taken on and butchered the Incredible Hulk. Had I not been so worried about him getting arrested, I'd have pissed myself. That crew I'd got into gear with were absolutely shitting bricks. I bet the nurses ran out of diapers on that ward that night.

To understand Dad's reaction, you have to understand what makes him tick. He is a fiercely proud man and ferociously protective of his family. He has an old-fashioned streak of fairness and a sense of honour. That's why, when I walked in that day with a blackeye, he made me face Jamie, rather than deal with it himself. The fact that I failed him on that occasion is a mere detail. He had played it fair.

When a much bigger, grown man punched and stamped on his teenage son, Dad absolutely flipped. That wasn't a fair fight. If it had been one of the kids I'd been fighting with, you can be sure he'd have lined up a rematch but it wasn't. My dad would have willingly done time over that bastard.

You cannot take liberties with the old lad either and woe betide anyone who bothers or embarrasses Mum or him when he's in her company. I remember Mum coming home looking worried one night – not by anything Dad had done to her; he wouldn't lay a finger on a woman, no matter what. It was down to something that he'd done to another bloke. She probably imagined the cops turning up at the door any minute to lock him up for GBH.

What had happened was this: they had been out for the

night at a local pub and Dad had bought a winning coupon that he had put in his back pocket. Some smartarse snatched it as he walked past him at the bar. Mum's recall of what happened next is a bit hazy because Dad reacted in a blur of action. A brief exchange of mumbled angry words as Mum headed to her seat caused her to turn and...'Derek, noooo! 'Too late! – *Kerr-runch!* Dad is a head-butt specialist.

The bridge of the pickpocket's nose broke on impact and his nostrils exploded; there was blood and snot from there to yonder. Then he was sent reeling under a hail of punches that left him in a heap on the pub floor. Now you might think that my dad had overreacted but you weren't there and don't live where we do. That's how it is and how hard-men, especially from his era, dealt with anyone who took the piss. The guy was either stupid or trying it on. Just maybe he thought that, with age, Decca Heggie Snr was there for the taking; a scalp that would jack up his own street cred.

Either way, he'd compounded his mistake by pulling that stunt in front of a pub full of folk dad knew *but*, worse still, with Mum there as well. *Tssk!* Bad idea. Dad has a well-earned rep around Carlisle and this muppet was disrespecting him in front of his wife. He could not let that go without doing something. Word would have soon got around; his standing in the hierarchy of tough guys would have been diminished. Before long, other up-and-coming hard cases would try to dig him out, just to be the guy who could boast, 'I done Decca Heggie in the other day.' No doubt a lot of you reading this book will recognise that mentality and, if you don't, you've led very sheltered life.

That night that I ended up in hospital has always stuck in my memory because it proved a great learning curve. When the big fella caught up with us, I hesitated. I admit I was scared 'cause I hadn't expected to see any of them again. That gave him an edge he didn't need. I'm not saying I'd have done him had I got stuck right into him straight away but at least it would have given me a fighting chance. As it was, I went down without landing a shot and he made sure that I stayed down. These days, if I saw a bloke doing that to a kid, I would break his jaw and make him beg for mercy before I'd stop.

Looking around that ward was an eye-opener. Apart from knocking Jamie out, who, let's face it, had banked a fuckin' good hiding 'with interest' years ago, that was the first time that I saw, first-hand, the results of my handiwork. Three lads, all older than I was at the time, lying on gurneys and in hospital beds. Shiners here, bust lips there, a couple of fractured jaws. I'd done quite a decent job on them and was well chuffed. How the hell I didn't appear in court I'll never know. They probably got told to say nothing by the big bastard, in case I made a counter complaint. No chance. I was happy to leave him to the old fella. Far greater punishment awaited him than any magistrates could dish out and it was served cold.

Sitting there on that gurney, it suddenly dawned on me just how hard a kid I had turned into and how hard a man I might end up being, having witnessed everyone quake at the sight of my dad's fury. Another fourteen years would pass before I truly found out. It seemed to be in such sharp contrast to the life I had led as a frightened boy. It just goes to show that the die is not cast. Unless, that is, you accept that being a victim is your lot in life.

Are you frightened? Do you live in fear? Let me tell you something I've learned about fear: it needn't necessarily be a negative thing. Straight up, I'm always frightened as I wait to face an opponent. When the knock comes and it's time to step into that ring and get it on, my guts are in a knot but a long time ago I learned to control fear and, eventually, I mastered it. Note that I use the word mastered, not denied or defeated. I don't think anyone who is being honest ever truly overcomes fear. We just handle it in different ways. I grew up with fear, you see, but fear is like an ally now.

Fear of those bullies became a fear of losing face with my dad. It's not easy being the eldest son of a well-known and respected local hard-man. After I shed the puppy-fat and grew stronger and harder, it became a fear of losing, be it at football or fighting. Then I began to utilise my fear and turn it into a form of motivation. When I made the leap from street-fighter to bouncer and on to become an unlicensed fighter, I harnessed that fear of losing to push myself harder during training sessions. Fear sharpened my responses and fighting instincts. Fear honed my natural ability and encouraged me to learn new martial skills.

So, you see, fear can be your friend. It's a leveller; a natural reaction to the unknown, to the threat of violence and the likelihood of pain. The important thing is not to let fear overcome you but to treat it more as a cautious friend whispering in your ear. Heed your fears but never let them rule you or you'll spend your life cowering or running and hiding.

We live in an era of unrealistic expectation, which, in itself, stokes unnecessary fears. I don't mean there is no chance of achieving your goals – quite the opposite actually. I truly believe we all can but what we can't do is perform miracles. I blame the media and particularly celebs or at least the culture that worshipping them has produced. Kids, in particular, can't seem to be able to see through the hype and bollocks. It's amazing what you can do with enough cash, a good surgeon or a fuckin' airbrush after a photo-shoot. Instead of kidding yourself that you can be the next catwalk queen, film star, *X-Factor* winner or reality-TV sensation, you should focus on making the most of what you have. Trust me: you'll achieve a lot more than you imagine you can.

Fact! All you can take with you when you die is the love of others but what you leave behind, that's down to you, mate. Don't say, 'I can't,' but, 'I can if I really try – if I truly believe and provided I don't give up.'

I'm up for it from the minute a fight is arranged. By the time I step into the arena, I'm utterly 100 per cent focused, be it a ring or backroom, a dingy yard or square of bales. The truth is I don't care. If the purse is worth the price of the pain, I'll fight anyone, anywhere. Once I've tapped fists with my opponent, all those hours of fitness training, pumping iron, bag work and sparring are tested and those ancient innate fight-or-flight instincts unleashed. There is nowhere to run, though. Not that I would, so fuck it! Let's fight.

At least that is how I go about things these days. Preparation for my first ever bareknuckle fight bore no resemblance to that routine. In fact, only four weeks before, I was on death's door having crashed and burned on an absolute mega cocaine binge that stopped my heart. Had the staff at the Cumberland Infirmary in Carlisle not kick-started me again, it really would have been curtains for Decca Jnr. They even called a priest. It proved a critical turning point for me so I'll come back to that tale later.

Having been discharged from hospital, I was moping around at home watching YouTube clips of bareknuckle fights and, after a while, I started thinking, 'I reckon I could take most of these fellas.' So I did a little research and phoned a bloke called Tucker Thompson. Next thing you know, I'm booked by B-Bad Promotions to take on Tony 'The Leicester Bulldog' Goward, a true veteran of the bareknuckle circuit, and in only three weeks' time. What the fuck had I done? I'd only agreed to an illegal bareknuckle fight with a guy who had been around the block more times than the postman's van – bollocks!

Three bleedin' weeks and there was I, still recovering from a near-death experience. The mirror told me all I needed to know about my readiness to enter my first bareknuckle bout. Overweight, out of condition, out of practice and out of my fuckin' mind, it seemed. Ah, well, it was too late. I'd said I'd fight and that was what I was going to do. OK, better get some roadwork in and clear my system of whatever shit still remained after the doctors had finished flushing me out. And that was all the training I did. Three weeks of pounding the pavements and footpaths around Old Harraby and beyond. No bag work, no gym sessions, just long, lung-busting runs.

What the hell was I thinking? Unless my fight strategy included outrunning Bulldog, it occurred to me that I'd better knock some of this ring-rust off and get some sparring done. With the fight less than two weeks away, only one name sprung to mind: Gary Dixon. Gary is a very tasty and experienced ex-pro boxer from Currock Villa Boxing Club and a really good bloke. I gave him a call and he said, 'No problem, Decca, man. Get yourself down here.' Brilliant. No sooner said than I was in the ring and testing my raw talent against his carefully crafted skills but, in no time, I got cocky and started taking liberties.

Sparring has its own etiquette but I wasn't following

it, partly out of ignorance and a little out of arrogance. Knowing I had a knockout punch, I started going in a bit heavy and Gary, quite understandably, got a little pissed off. He didn't say anything but countered my pile-drivers while upping his game.

Gary, mate, I take my hat off to you: a true gent, a sport and a great teacher. Lesson learned. He gave me three rounds of hell and put me well and truly in my place by knocking seven bells out of me. When we were done, he explained the rules of sparring and told me where I'd gone wrong but added that his door was always open. No hard feelings. Top man.

Come the day of the fight, me, my cousin Johnny, Pete Irwin, Steve Jardine and Billy Miller just jumped into the car and sped off down to Dave Courtney's house, 'Camelot' in south London. Actually, poor Billy went the whole friggin' way in the boot! Billy moved to Brighton not long after. He's a bit on the skinny side, to be honest, but what he lacks in size he makes up for in attitude. Quite a dangerous little bastard to get on the wrong side of is Billy.

Courtney's gaff: that in itself is an experience. Dave is a larger-than-life underworld 'face' and former enforcer. Think of a famous name from London's gangland scene and Dave Courtney will know him (or have known him if he has since been 'starred up' to that prison beyond the Pearly Gates) and, likely as not, has their numbers in his phone. This geezer's better connected than fibre-optic broadband. He was even a good mate of my childhood hero Lenny McLean, the lucky bastard. I would have loved to have met that fighting legend.

Dave made us feel very welcome and turned out to be a proper funny bloke. When I say funny, I mean tears streaming, sides aching, hysterically so, which was a tad unexpected and a touch surreal, considering his dark and dangerous past. Talk about flamboyant: that guy's a total showman and nothing reflects his eccentric side better than his house. It occupies what was once the east wing of a former Victorian-built school. It's a big, brash, gloriously over-the-top temple to crime and it's extravagant – oh yeah, and then some.

Murals and heraldic insignia decorate the walls and the whole gable end is a group-portrait tribute to the men he most admires. Joey Pyle's up there with Roy Shaw, Lenny McLean, Tony Lambrianou and Charlie Richardson, and with a 'yours truly, Mr C' seated on a throne in the middle. It's the business and all painted by two blokes from my neck of the woods up in Cumbria. Trust me: this is not the home of a man who tries to stay off the police radar and quietly go about his business. It screams, 'Here I am and here I'll stay, so what the fuck are you gonna do about it?'

Why am I telling you all this? Because I was fighting The Leicester Bulldog in the former gangster's back garden. I know – bizarre, eh! We'd barely been there ten minutes before the ref called us together. Good job I travelled down wearing my fighting gear and phoned ahead to secure a decent corner man 'cause I didn't really have any idea what I was getting into. Sean Smith (aka 'Britain's Deadliest Debt-Collector') had stepped up for me. How did he come by that title? What can I say? Sean can be very, very persuasive. Let's put it this way: if you owe someone a wedge and Sean comes knocking to collect, pay the man. I knew that, with him in my corner, my back – and the purse – was safe. Not that I need have worried. As it turned out, like all 'Old School' underworld geezers, Dave Courtney wouldn't have stood for me being rumped on his manor either.

Having barely caught my breath, I found myself tapping knuckles with a big, burly bruiser whose scar tissue had scar tissue. The sound of the bell heralded a brutal thirteen-minute exchange of punching power that felt more like thirteen hours. Believe me: when The Leicester Bulldog is laying into you, thirteen seconds seems like a lifetime.

He's not what you'd call athletically built but don't be deceived: Tony's some unit. He's got staying power too and skills galore. He has fists like mallets with ball-bearings for knuckles, fixed onto the ends of a set of arms a silverback gorilla would be proud of and powered by a pair of bulky, rolling shoulders.

I relied entirely on strength, adrenaline, street-fighting *nous* and the limited experience I'd gleaned on the unlicensed circuit, whereas Tony had been a bareknuckle fighter for as long as I had been alive. He pressed forward more like a bulldozer than a bulldog and slammed some perfectly aimed shots into my head and face. He rocked me a few times and even had me on the bales once. Youth, energy and raw aggression prevailed along with my inbuilt refusal to lose. Eventually, I overpowered that awesome veteran with a series of solid shots of my own. Some severe damage was done. We both bled but I won.

Tony's a genuine fella, a really lovely bloke and a legend on the bareknuckle scene; a guy who had his first fight at only thirteen years of age. Even then, he took on a lad four years older than him and held him to a draw over ninety minutes. Imagine that: one and a half hours. That's not a fight, it's a war of attrition. How many thirteen-year-olds do you know that could handle that sort of punishment? Never mind that: how many do you know that would take on a seventeen-year-old in their first straightener?

Tony did and he took that kid on twice more. The second time, the cheating twat hit Tony with a half-brick but, at their final rematch and with a score to settle, a seventeen-year-old Tony Goward put the fucker away with just two punches of pure quality. The game little pup from Leicester had grown into a pit-fighting Bulldog.

Take it from me: this straight-talking, no-nonsense, fighting gentleman known as 'The Leicester Bulldog' is a class act. Despite being in his early forties when we met, Tony proved a formidable opponent, especially for a bareknuckle novice like me. He's a bone-fide hard bastard whose fists can punch holes in you. At least that's what it feels like when you're on the receiving end. If this fella is facing you in a fight, you've got huge problems. But if you ever find yourself in a tight corner and Tony's got your back, you've got nothing to worry about.

The 'Clash at Camelot' was a real baptism of fire for me and the start of a winning streak that saw me claim two national BKB heavyweight-title belts and the most prized title in the fight game, The Guv'nor.

CHAPTER FOUR

B-BAD
TIMES

All too often, kids from my sort of background, who have their whole lives ahead of them, flush it down the toilet. Why? I blame the government. No, bear with me. They offer no real hope. Oh yeah, they're all there with their catchy little sound-bites and telling us what they have accomplished 'in real terms.' What the fuck does that mean? I'm no linguistic expert but, surely, real means – real. What terms can you put on what is real? In my book, it either *is* or it *isn't*. I don't know about you but, to me, it stinks of bullshit.

I don't watch a lot of news programmes but enough to have become completely cynical. I'm sick of hearing prime ministers telling us what a bang-up job he or she is doing creating jobs. Really? Do you suppose they'd ever stick their precious kids into one of those minimum-wage dead-end jobs on a zero-hours contract? Would they fuck!

The kids of these same politicians get a leg up from day

one, doors opened and red carpets rolled out for them wherever they go. Kids from my walk of life get shown the school gates when our education ends and are then left to our own devices. I'm on safe political ground here because I'm speaking as a lad who could never hold down even the most menial of jobs. If you ask me, though, I've just highlighted the reason I couldn't: in a word – menial. Every job I ever applied for – which wasn't many, I admit – was so mind-numbingly boring that I'd be praying they'd bin the form. When I did finally get a job, after only one week the gaffer got me so pissed off that I chased him around the yard and was going to smash his head in with the pressure washer I'd been using. I got the sack, of course. Apparently, I excelled at pissing employers off. It's in my CV. My dad went round to see the twat at his farm but he wouldn't open the door, so he was a coward and a twat – but maybe not a stupid coward and twat. To summarise: in 'real terms', those politicians are just talking out of their arses.

Don't worry: I've pushed my soap box back under my bed. I'll leave all that bollocks for you to mull over while I tell you how I screwed up my future big time without any help from the government. But it all began with piss-poor employment prospects – and glue.

Nowadays, I look back and cringe at my own stupidity. Life is a series of ups and downs. One minute you're high, then your low, and it's no different when you're a junkie, whether its addiction to solvents or controlled drugs. But unlike life's highs and lows, these are massively exaggerated swings; more like soaring and plummeting. Because the coming down is so grim that, as quick as you can, you're back on your chosen poison. Get the picture? Take my advice. If anyone ever suggests trying any controlled substance, or even these so-called 'legal highs', run a fuckin' mile.

The thing that really bugs me now, as I write about these things, is that I was a pretty switched-on kid and yet I fell for that old line: 'Curious, Decca, mate? Here, try it. What harm can it do?'

Like an idiot who knew no better, I did. The worst decision of my life was when I first began inhaling solvents. Do you know what? I fuckin' loved that first fuzzy rush; unlike other drugs I went on to try, it lingered for quite a while. Next thing you know, I'm a fuckin' bag-head, sneaking off with the other wasters and losers to gas up or sniff on whatever we could lift. Mention the words drug addict and most people immediately think of heroin and shit like that. Trust me: everyday solvent-based products are no less addictive.

They quickly became my 'go-to' solution for everything and anything that was bothering me. They opened my mind to trying other sorts of highs and buzzes. Bored, Decca? Why not buy or nick some glue, bag it, breathe it in and get off your tits? Off I would go – sorted. By nick, I mean either steal the money or the glue. A chicken-and-egg scenario. What came first? I'm ashamed to say, sneakily nicking money from my mum's purse or my dad's jacket pocket. Nicking glue or gas or aerosols always came with the risk of getting locked up for shoplifting but I resorted to that as well when there was no ready cash lying around the house.

Next thing you know, I was caught in a spiral of thieving and getting off my face. Around the back of Harraby Community Centre was our preferred place for bagging-up and getting high but it's a habit you can satisfy in just about anywhere that's reasonably private. That kind of behaviour leads to nothing but trouble. What would I do when trouble came calling? Bag some more or snort a can of solvent, an extinguisher or an aerosol and all the trouble would go away. Yeah, right. Until I came back down again to find that, while off my scope, I had done something else that was even more monumentally insane than the thing I was escaping from in the first place.

Downers became part of that cycle as well, so I'd do even more. How was I to know that the downs that were occurring with increasing frequency were a side effect of the highs? The chemicals I was ingesting were fuckin' up my brain. I'm absolutely certain it was that period of heavy solvent abuse that slipped that Black Dog from its leash.

Somehow, I had kept a lid on it through the bullying era of my childhood, probably thinking the bad feelings would lift once it stopped. Using the glue and stuff definitely brought it out. The bugger really bit with a vengeance as I moved into adulthood. To this day, it still troubles me from time to time. Alcohol fuelled my aggression and left me with hangovers but solvents messed my head up completely. Oddly enough, even as I grew increasingly addicted to these substances, I continued to improve and progress as a soccer player.

It was around this time that I first met the man who now manages me, Alan 'Macca' McDermott. Macca and my dad go back a long way and regularly met in the St Nicholas Arms after their respective training sessions. Macca coached junior rugby league players and Dad managed our soccer team. He knew my dad on account of his reputation and Dad knew the craic about him as well. It was a mutual respect thing, because, truth be told, Macca's no slouch in a tear-up.

He was one of the founder members of Carlisle United's

notorious hooligans, the BCF (Border City Firm). Now you may be appalled by that or scoff at the thought of Carlisle United having a 'firm' but, for a small crew, the BCF punched way above their weight whenever they clashed with rival firms from bigger clubs and Macca was always in the thick of the action. He ended up getting remanded in custody over a football-violence related incident but shouldn't have even been charged. However, that's his story to tell, not mine. You can see how a lad like him and a bloke like my old lad would get on, though, eh? They both loved a good ruck and both loved football.

Like Dad, though, come his day in court, Macca learned who his true friends were after some BCF lads gave evidence that condemned him. As a result and while on remand, he learned an important and salutary lesson and has walked a straight path ever since. After his trial and return to Carlisle as a free man, he walked away from that life and took up playing rugby league and proved to be a natural. He went on to represent his county and Ireland as an amateur international. Once his playing days were over, he became a junior coach. The man wanted to put something back into the sport that had given him so much and also to help steer youngsters away from the sort of trouble that saw him lose his liberty.

Whatever you think of his past, Alan McDermott is a proper decent and honest man and I, like many others, am proud to call him my friend.

When Macca clapped eyes on me for the first time, he tried to poach me. He saw potential in me playing rugby league, being as how I had shaped up and filled out. For a fifteen-year-old, I was a very physical kid; fast as well as strong. I was flattered by his interest but swapping the round ball for an oval one was never gonna happen.

By then, I'd also become the youngest ever player to play in the Northern Football Alliance and was offered a trial at Derby County but never followed through on that opportunity. I felt that I was too young and Derby seemed such a long, long way from home. Instead, I was signed by Workington Reds under-seventeens and played against Newcastle in the FA Youth Cup. From Workington I transferred to Tarf Rovers in Scotland but didn't really enjoy my time up there never really settled into the side. Then I picked up a serious hamstring injury that prematurely ended my playing career. Such is the nature of competitive sport, especially physical contact sports. Injury is a constant threat, and never more so than in a pit <line space> Taking on and beating a fighter with the skills and experience of the Leicester Bulldog was a massive boost to my confidence. It also brought home to me my many shortcomings: there is no room in the unforgiving sport of bareknuckle boxing for any sort of weakness. Another bonus came in the form of a bloke I met down there, Colin Wood – a man who has since become a true friend. At the time, Colin was doing a lot of work for Knuckle Promotions, which is owned by a big name in Big Knockout Boxing (BKB), James Quinn McDonagh, who I'll speak of in greater detail later. Nowadays, Colin promotes disabled events through his own promotions company, Wheeled Warriors.

The pit-fighting and bareknuckle world is a bit of a jungle, which literally crawls with snakes, some of them quite deadly. Colin was an experienced promoter and he could see that, being so naïve, I was vulnerable to the vipers that were already circling me. Having consulted with my dad, Colin took me under his wing. He invited me down to his place in Warwickshire, where I stayed for six months and was treated like one of the family.

It was during this time that a fight in Wales, of all places, with a so-called hard-man from Millwall was arranged. This geezer, to refer to his character type as he would himself, was a former member of F-Troop – or was it Bushwacker? Either way, he was once a Millwall FC football hooligan. I wonder if he and Macca ever crossed paths in those bad old days? Probably not as it was a different era but Millwall had a notorious following and the BCF loved nothing better than testing themselves against a rival firm with a tasty rep.

Whoever and whatever he was, I was up for it but the buzz surrounding the fight brought one of the most venomous of snakes out from the undergrowth. Joe Smith-Brown is a proper smooth operator. A man who wormed his way into Colin's circle and quickly became a friend. Yeah, right.

Joe was looking for a way into the bareknuckle scene and he saw a gullible rookie like me as the perfect means to that end. He offered sponsorship and threw money my way and volunteered to set up a fan page. All good stuff and, in no time at all, Joe had his feet under the table and was part of the team. As it turned out, the fight never actually happened.

That disappointment was soon assuaged by Joe, who seemed too good to be true. I took him at face value and befriended the man. Within a few short weeks, Joe Smith-Brown had his key to the BKB door – me. He was a player overnight. The next thing you know he's a partner in B-Bad Promotions and, not long after, had adopted the moniker Joe B-Bad. Bad by name and worse by nature – much worse.

Joe Smith-Brown (aka Joe B-Bad): I have waited so long

to tell my side of the story about that c**t. It started back in February 2014. I can still recall the conversation I had on the phone with him as if it was yesterday. It came while I was staying at Colin Wood's flat in Warwickshire.

At this point, I want to make one thing absolutely clear: Colin is one of the few genuine people I have met during my short time on the bareknuckle scene – no strings and no hidden agenda. Colin let me stay with him, rent free, for six months while I was training down there. To this day, he remains a trusted friend of both me and my dad. Almost single-handedly, this gentleman launched Wheeled Warriors as a means to get disabled people who wanted to compete into combat sport. This is not a scheme that will ever make him rich: it costs him money but he devotes his every waking hour to it and his people. That's the kind of diamond bloke I'm talking about.

A few other snakes in the game would have people believe that he's not to be trusted. I want everyone who reads this book to know and to tell their friends that Colin Wood is a genuinely decent man. Take that as the God's honest truth from the Guv'nor himself.

Joe knew Colin as a promoter. He wormed his way into Colin's confidence by telling him he would support his dream of getting his Wheeled Warriors project off the ground. Make no mistake: Joe's a very sharp feller with a very convincing line in patter. What neither of us realised at the time, though, was that *I* was Joe's prime target. He used Colin to get to me and no sooner did he have his friendship than he offered to sponsor me to the sum of £500.

What is not bullshit is that Joe was, and still is, a very wealthy and successful businessman. He owns an accountancy firm in Oxford, among other things. Joe arranged, through

Colin, to meet me in Northampton but, instead, turned up at Colin's place and took me for a craic over a steak and a pint of coke. It didn't take him long to get to the point. He wanted to be my manager.

What was not in question was his business brain, eagerness and enthusiasm. What else is a novice fighter looking for in a potential manager? He'd driven all the way from Oxford to make his pitch. If I signed up with him, he would fund my living and training expenses, as well as steer my career all the way to the top of the game. 'Pinch me, I'm dreaming,' I thought.

Joe was saying all the things I wanted to hear. Being so far from home, my dad wasn't around to give any advice and, although Macca had become a close confidante, he wasn't actively involved in that scene. It sounded like a win-win situation for both me and Joe. I was greener than the Jolly Green Giant and nearly as big: with a firm and welcome handshake, the deal was sealed.

Things got off to a good start. Joe was as good as his word, paying £300 a week into my bank account for me to live off and treating me with respect – more like a good mate than a client. We used to go off on days out together. We'd have a right laugh and yet I was totally unaware of the real reasons behind his support and friendship. As a manager, it put him front and centre when dealing with promoters: owning his own promotions company was where his ambitions really lay.

At this stage, I still only had the one fight under my belt, with Tony Goward, The Leicester Bulldog. It was Joe who lined up a fight with the tough guy from Millwall. In preparation for this, my second bareknuckle bout, I'd been training hard and weighed in at eighteen stone by the time the bout came around, which, for me, was a decent fighting weight. It was only my second fight, so I was pretty nervous and even more so when we got there.

The arena had been setup in what's best described as a hut, and not a very big one at that. They had marked out the eight-by-eight foot fighting pit with hay bales. It wasn't as if I was expecting New York Coliseum but this was strictly no frills; proper grassroots stuff. Any more basic and we may as well have fought in a back-alley or on any old piece of common ground.

Bollocks to it: I wasn't bothered. I was eager to test myself again, so I got my hands strapped and began warming up. By that time my opponent – a big lad called Ben something or other – had arrived. The trouble was that the changing and warm-up area was so small and so crowded that we found ourselves sharing the same cramped space. I wasn't concerned about what he was up to but Ben had clocked me slamming the pads. I don't mind admitting I was feeling sharp and my confidence was growing by the minute. He must have bottled it or the cold, hard reality of bareknuckle fighting suddenly came to him. All of a sudden, he walked over to me and told me he didn't want to fight. I was stunned.

I stood looking at him in disbelief and maybe gasped something like, 'For fuck's sake, are you taking the piss? '

I'd spent three hours on the road travelling from Warwickshire for this straightener. Not only that but Decca Snr, bless him, had come all the way down from Carlisle to watch his boy in action. The Millwall Muppet just shrugged, grabbed his gear and fucked off back to London. What sort of feller signs up for a fight and backs out before a punch is thrown? A shithouse, that's who!

I bet he thought he was going to be taking on some wannabe

chump from up north. There is this attitude that pervades among some down south that us lads from the far north are all sheep-shagging country bumpkins, whereas they're all well-hard geezers with street-smarts and a Ray Winstone growl. Wrong. I kinda hope I've gone some way to changing that attitude in the past three years and, remember, as I said at the start, I'm not even the hardest in my family.

Straight up, I could take you on a Cumbria Tough Guys Bus Tour and introduce you to some proper hard lads from every corner my home county. I'd back them against quite a few of the tastier blokes I've met along the way.

So anyway, the whole business proved a real anti-climax. I walked away with a measly £250 for my trouble by way of compensation – not much of a return on the time and effort I'd put into preparing for the fight. Back to the drawing board and back into my training regime. In total, Joe managed me for twelve months and in that time only got me two other fights, both of which were in America.

As time passed under his management, I began to question his strategy and wonder (a) if he even had one, and (b) why he didn't seem to want me to fight in my own country. The reason was simple: at that time, B-Bad Promotions' owner was a bloke called Andy Topliffe and he looked after the interests of rival fighters. Joe had been schmoozing and acting a bit flash around Andy, making out what a great manager he was and what a great asset he could be to the game. It paid off when Andy asked if he wanted to buy 50 per cent of his company.

Now Andy Topliffe is just as big a snake as Joe but, on his part, it was sound business, nothing more. He knew Joe had money and nearly all these fringe-sport promotion outfits are run on a shoe-string. Taking Joe on as a partner meant sharing the costs and the hassle involved in running the business and it would bring in a much needed injection of operating capital. All well and good, you would think. Not for everyone.

Joe phoned me and said, 'Listen, Decca. Andy's offered me a half-share in B-Bad and I thought I'd run it by you, mate.'

What did he expect me to say but 'Yeah, go for it, mate'?

Joe went on to tell me at length how he was buying into B-Bad to boost my career and how he was going to stay on as my manager; how he still wanted the best for me. I believed him. That's what managers are supposed to do and, up to that point, he had been funding my living and training expenses. So I was left thinking, 'What a great guy I've got on my team. He's bought a fuckin' company to ensure my success.'

Having gone in as a fifty-fifty partner, Joe was soon telling me that, within a couple of months, he would own the lot. That's how a ruthless, ambitious and shrewd businessman like him operates. Half of something is better than none but all of it is best.

Around August 2014 I got a phone call from B-Bad Promotions. It was Joe. He'd got me another fight – in America again. Joe had been my manager for six months by now and, even with the weight of his newly acquired company behind him, I was yet to fight in the UK under his management.

The fight – my second in Philadelphia – was arranged but I then discovered he'd also arranged an event in Wales, from which I was excluded. My manager was arranging bareknuckle events but not putting me on the ticket. When I challenged him about it, he said that he was worried I'd get hurt. Have you ever heard anything so stupid? Who did he think he was talking to: some pussy of a prima donna? I'm a former street-fighter, an unlicensed fighter and a fuckin' bareknuckle fighter for Christ's sake! Getting hurt goes with the job. Did he think me and the hard American bastard across the pond were gonna be swatting each other with cheerleaders' pom-poms?

It took me far too long to realise that he wasn't promoting me. Holding me back only benefitted my rivals and their managers. Whose side was he on? Was this raw warrior from Carlisle with no pedigree in danger of scuppering their plans? I'd gained notoriety, having become a bit of an overnight sensation when I burst onto the scene at Dave Courtney's gaff. It's the only explanation I can come up with that makes any kind of sense, and I've given the matter a lot of thought. Consider this: these people had invested time and money in guys that had been around a lot longer than me; carefully building reps and growing a following. Then I appear on YouTube in the 'Clash at Camelot'. All of a sudden, I'm of interest, despite my lack of fights. There is no denying that there was a real buzz around the circuit about this new kid on the block. What I've never understood is how Joe and his so-called friend didn't pick up on that vibe. Did he take his eye off the ball? Or was his eye set on another prize from the outset? Beats me.

I went to the States with Joe and Aaron 'Popeye' Watts, who had been guiding Joe since he bought into B-Bad. This was my second trip to Philadelphia, having put Eric Ward away on a previous visit with one punch. That's all you need to know about that fight. I flew to America, knocked out a Yank, collected the purse and flew back. For all the time that took we may as well have arranged the fight on the tarmac at PHL Airport and asked the pilot to keep the engine running.

Because of the Welsh thing I was not in the best frame

of mind when I arrived in the US but I relaxed in my usual way by checking my Facebook page. As usual, Joe had been busy wheeling and dealing, making calls and taking calls, but something wasn't right. I could tell by his hushed tones and one-word responses. Then I got wind of a suspicion that the fight had been rigged. I was fucking fuming.

Ultimately, I do not know if it was true or not, but there's no way I'd ever get involved in such a thing. Get me a proper fight or get me on the next flight out of here,' I said, and that's what happened. Joe didn't like that but, sure enough, another fighter was arranged. Not that he proved any harder to beat than the guy that had been willing to take a dive. On reflection, I think that was where the rot set into our partnership. I always had niggling doubts about the whole B-Bad set-up after that and Joe was never quite the same with me either.

Now Bobby Gunn claims to be the World Bareknuckle Champion and it took him ten minutes to defeat the same guy that I was about to fight next. Sorry but I can't even remember his name and it's a wonder because it was a memorable fight but not in the way you might imagine. It took me fractionally over three minutes to win and that's including several pauses while the guy caught his breath. Bobby Gunn, World Champ, as measured by that particular opponent: I remain unconvinced.

As bareknuckle fighters go, my opponent wasn't the biggest I'd ever tackled but I had been warned that he was a very experienced boxer with real fast hand speed and that he'd stood his ground against Bobby 'World Champ' Gunn for ten minutes. So I was expecting a hard fight. What I hadn't expected was that he'd spend half the fight almost bent double, trying to get under or avoid my punches, or that he'd throw one shot for about every ten I delivered.

I'm what you might call a semi-crouch fighter; back slightly bent, shoulders hunched, chin tucked. This bugger was circling me at a right-angle to the floor. I couldn't make my mind up whether he was trying to fight me or give me a blow job. Stand-up fight? Any lower and we'd have been fighting on our hands and knees. At one minute, fifteen seconds, he went down. Not long after, he actually wrapped his arms around my fuckin' thigh, for Christ's sake. I'd had and seen boxers hang on but never to someone's leg. I stuck to the task and kept swinging but my blows were glancing off the back of his head. What else could I do? I'd have had to have been lying flat on my back to hit him in the face.

Coming up to the two-minute mark, I'd barely seen his face and, a few seconds later, he stepped out of the square for a breather. No, not a count, a fuckin' breather! Then the fight resumed and, at three minutes and thirty-five seconds, after taking a couple more solid shots to the mush on one of those rare occasions when he did raise his head, he'd had enough. I'd done the business but no thanks to Popeye. He had bound my hands so tightly that they had started to go numb with the fight barely underway – and that is dangerous. Lack of circulation in a bareknuckle bout can result in serious damage to the hands and what good is a bareknuckle fighter with knackered fists? Talk about a botched job.

On the topic of Popeye, it seemed that he had been whispering in Joe's ear for quite a while that he should ditch me. For whatever reason, Popeye didn't rate me or see me as a prospect. I think Joe had begun to believe him but, for a while, was torn over whether to let me go or not. If I'd broken my hands in that fight in Philly, that would have been the end for me and Joe would have been left with no choice but to write me off. Thankfully, I didn't but I returned the UK and headed back to Carlisle still brooding about being left off the bill at that Welsh BKB event.

As a consequence of that, and Joe's relative inaction regards managing my career, relations became a little strained. He continued to slither his way around the BKB scene, making connections and working hard on raising his, and B-Bad's, profile while inexplicably holding me back. Calls became less frequent. It was always me trying to pin him down to try to get me a fight arranged but nothing ever happened.

It became increasingly obvious that B-Bad Promotions was all about Joe Smith-Brown and his enormous ego. Oh yeah, it was a promotions company all right; one that exclusively promoted the cause and BKB credibility of its owner, full-stop. I truly believe the dickhead feared that I would end up bigger than him or his promotion company. Well, guess what? He was right!

Furthermore, I had sensed from early on that Popeye was jealous of my friendship with Joe but can only speculate on his motives. What was evident was the influence he had over Joe. To my mind, it was all very underhand, unpleasant and totally unnecessary. BKB is about fighting and you would think a promoter would consider any decent prospect a valuable asset and treat them accordingly. Apparently not – I was brushed aside. Not even a nearly man – a barely-got-started man. He wasted my time and quite a bit of his own money, more fool him, but I was not finished. No way. I had only just begun.

Regardless of whoever and whatever was behind the rift, it led to a complete breakdown of trust and, in the end, our parting ways, though mutual, left a bitter taste. I had my reasons for walking away but Joe's remain a mystery. He's entitled to his opinion of me as a fighter but, until he puts the best he's got from his stable up against me, I reserve the right to tell him to put up or shut up. Better still – fuck off.

As Joe B-Bad's 'former client', my record speaks for itself. With the UK, EBF and Guv'nor titles to my name, from here on in I dictate the terms, or at least Macca does. Now there's a guy who could teach that arsehole a thing or two about managing a fighter. In fact, the two that followed Joe could learn a lot from Macca, and don't worry: I will get around to them. Under Macca's careful stewardship, things have really started to happen. I no longer jump the minute some promotion company – especially Joe B-Bad's outfit – snap their fingers.

Not that Joe will. He hasn't got a fighter on his books that he'll risk in a ring or pit against The Guv'nor. Or has he? If you're reading this, Joe, never mind posting snide remarks on social-media sites or grubbing around for tired old craics and dirty laundry to hang out in a pathetic attempt to embarrass me: man up and meet me face-to-face.

I'm glad I've got that off my chest at long last but, for a quite a while after leaving B-Bad, things did not get better. All Joe B-Bad had done for me was organise two of the only three illegal fights I have ever participated in and both of those were in the United States. The fact I did that just shows how keen I was to prove myself and gain experience. Nowadays, I wouldn't even consider doing such a thing again but I'd entered that world a complete novice and with just about everyone who was involved in BKB doubting that I was made of the right stuff to make any impression.

Cast adrift but determined to grow as a fighter, in order to challenge for titles, I had to come up with a plan but, thanks to Joe, I didn't know who I could trust. Paranoia had set in and threatened to drag me back towards some very dark places.

CHAPTER FIVE

LOVE AND OTHER DRUGS

Finding myself without a manager plunged me into another deep depression but I took some comfort from the fact that I handled it better than I would have done in the past. There was no turning towards drugs and drink to ease my disappointment or escape the dark moods. I had grown. I had focus and a new goal. I just had to work harder and burn all that B-Bad shit out of my system; had to come up with a new game-plan and find another manager.

I've known very many low points in my time and this was yet another. It dragged up those old and unforgotten feelings of being friendless and alone against the world. Yeah, I know that sounds melodramatic but that's depression for you. Being in its clutches is a drama – a psycho-drama.

Such was the hope I'd attached to having Joe's hand to guide me that, when it all dissolved, I began to feel as I had done after losing someone else who had arrived in my life full of hope and promise. Her name was Becky. The only woman I have ever truly loved. I say woman; she was only sixteen when we met but she was no giggly, silly schoolgirl. Becky had an old, smart head on her.

I'd begun working on the doors at nineteen, having been taken on by a top bloke called Mike Grierson. Granny, as he's known, was a legend around Carlisle, having run most of the doors back in the day. He gave me my first start as a match steward at Brunton Park, Carlisle United's ground. Being unemployed and potless, I'd tapped him up for a job.

I was pretty well knocked together by then, bang into the steroids and a regular at the gym. It wasn't all about body image but I have to admit that I got a proper buzz out of filling my XXL shirts. My body shape might have changed but something that hasn't since I got into training is my determination, drive and focus. Whether it's distance running or sprints, pumping iron or bag-work, pads or sparring, I give 100 per cent. I love it. Nothing beats putting myself through a good, hard training session and pushing myself to the limit. Well, almost nothing but this book isn't called *Fifty Shades of Heggie*, so we won't go there.

During my preparation for The Guv'nor title fight the training regime I followed was intense but not rigid. It's all about getting the basics right really. Eat right; sleep well, preferably for a solid eight hours and do regular exercise. That's all anyone needs to stay fit. However, if you really want to improve or grow muscle you have to mix-things-up from time to time. Your body will soon get used to any repetitive routine and before long, will only be giving you what you need to get through it and no more. Every so often you should shock your system and the best way to do that is to introduce an exercise you haven't done for a while, or ever before for that matter. Once you start or even if you only hope to compete at a serious level, in any sport, you have to be disciplined about your diet, really step up your work rate in the gym and during cardio routines.

I was very lucky to secure the services of Ian 'Chem' Chambers. Not only did he put me through a punishing muscle-building routine but he also sorted me out a balanced medium-carb, high protein diet which was delivered to the gym as ready-made meals; a week's supply, boxed for me to take home. On top of that he was very generous with supplying protein and pre-workout supplements; he was brilliant. Over the space of a few months, thanks to his routine and diet, I became bulked, honed and toned.

At least four times a week I'd be out of bed around 5. 30am to get some food into me before I caught the train or bus to Whitehaven and, after warming up on a static bike or stair climber in an altitude mask to intensify the experience, spend forty minutes pumping iron. Chem would mix the exercises up but rarely ever, the combinations: chest and triceps one day, back and biceps another, shoulders often as not in isolation, as was my favourite routine, legs! I love doing legs and as the weeks passed they got massive and proper ripped.

Leg strength plays a big part in my fights. My best and often, knockout shots start at floor level. From the semi-crouch position I can launch a punch that starts from my back foot. Pushing off I transfer the power up through my leg in one fluid move into my lats and shoulder muscles before unleashing all that power and energy through my right arm and clenched fist, then – *boom!* Another opponent hits the dirt or canvas.

Chem's also a stickler for warm-ups and stretching first before easing into a routine but once we got going he'd push me all the way; relentless explosive routines to produce muscle and power. He'd start me off on really light weights and with each consecutive set (up to five or six) he'd steadily increase it until I'd max-out; such as on an inclined chest press at around 180kg and as high as 200kg shoulder pressing. (Having always had naturally broad and powerful shoulders, after legs, they have always been my strongest suit when it comes to pumping iron.) Chem'd keep the burn going by stripping the bar 20kg at a time, after I'd peaked, as I knocked out more reps, until we got back down to the starting weight. Whether it was on the Smith machine or any other, by the time you're back to the starting weight, every fibre of the target muscle area feels like it's on fire. And I absolutely love that sensation.

I'm never happier than when I'm working out on weight or a bag. For a feel-good rush, you cannot beat the release of endorphins.

Besides the four intense weight-training sessions, twice a week I was flipping heavy tractor tyres with Macca and doing plenty of roadwork. Five or six days a week I'd run five miles, that included some testing hill-climbs and often with one of those altitude masks on to make it feel like a half-marathon. I used to get some funny looks as I jogged along country lanes looking like a cross between Hannibal Lecter and The Hulk. As I built up the mileage and pace, at first, I'd get maybe half or two thirds of the way through the course before I'd have to drag the mask off but as the fight neared I was getting really fit and able to keep it on until the final two-hundred yards where I'd burst into a finishing sprint.

My bag-work and sparring sessions were a bit more hit-and-miss and, as the fight got closer, were a source of growing frustration to be honest. Macca tried to fix me up with a couple of sparring partners but what they offered by way of knowledge, skills and ability, they lacked in consistency. One day they'd be keen as mustard, the next making excuses and trying to reschedule or just not returning our calls. That sort of attitude is no use when you're facing a former pro-heavyweight like Louis Francis. Being a boxing coach himself, he was getting plenty of bag-work, ring-work and sparring sessions under his belt in readiness.

As for staying sharp; I can go three minute rounds on the bag with the statutory 'corner' breaks all day long and work a speed-ball with the best of them. Unfortunately I was let down on that front more than once as well and didn't get as much time on the bag or pads as I would have liked. Eventually though, I got into some regular sparring and pad sessions with Mark Hodgson from Workington who has his own martial arts school. He helped sharpen me up and taught me a few neat offensive and counter-offensive moves.

Since bringing the title belt home I've lightened up on my weights routine but knock out a lot more reps. Heavy or light, I train to failure; it's the only way to get the best out of yourself and create quality muscle.

I think I can safely say that when it comes to preparation for a fight, I'm up there with any professional in my level of commitment and willingness to push myself to the limit and beyond. A word of caution: there are no short cuts or silver bullets to achieving success. You have to be ravenously hungry to be a champion and to take exercise to the extremes that I do. And I was – and as a result – I am!

Of course, Granny knew my Heggie pedigree and asked if I had any other ambitions beyond door work.

'Yeah, sure I have, Granny. Your job.'

I think my cocky response tickled him and he took me on. As was Granny's way, he worked alongside me for a few weeks to weigh me up and soon discovered that not only was I dependable in a ruck but capable of talking people down as well. That's what he was looking for: tough lads who could handle the aggro but didn't resort to the heavy stuff until all else had failed. Granny wouldn't tolerate or employ bullies and thugs who were just looking to get paid for battering anyone that got on their wick.

At the time, Granny's firm, Paramount Security, had the contract for loads of doors and we used to work wherever we were sent. In the early evening we'd work some of the pubs down Botchergate in Carlisle. It's one of the city's nightlife hot-spots and, as a consequence, trouble-spots. It's lined down both sides by pubs, bars and fast-food outlets. I'd find myself minding the door at The Cumberland Arms. It was a cracking old pub but it could get real feisty in there at a weekend. Or any number of others: The Old Crown, The Rambler and The Caledonian, to mention but three more. It could get pretty lively, I can tell you. As kicking-out time loomed, the pubs would empty and we'd move onto the night clubs. The same faces but with a lot more drink, drugs and attitude on board.

I usually got sent on to Legends but this particular night I was on the door at The Front Page when Becky walked up to the kiosk. I instantly knew that I had to be with her. She knew our Barry from school so I used that as my opener.

'Hello. I'm Decca. Barry's brother.' I said. After a gentle but persistent charm offensive, I persuaded her to share a taxi home and, during the journey, asked if we could meet again. She didn't believe I'd show so I gave her my sovereign ring. 'I'll be back for that tomorrow night and take you out.'

She was just everything I wanted in a girlfriend and, when I returned the following night, that's what she became. In no time we were an item and totally loved-up. I was absolutely crazy about her and she was into me big style. That was early 2002 and Becky and I were together for one all-too-short but unforgettable year.

Legends, better known to the previous generation as the Twisted Wheel, was a very popular night club on the city's ancient, defensive West Walls. It used to make me laugh to think that our ancestors fought off invaders on those same walls and that I often found myself scrapping with lads from over the border who would arrive by the bus load come the weekend, pissed up, revved up and well up for a bit of a ruck. I've thrown a few down the stone steps at Town Dyke or kicked their arses along the walls towards the viaduct. Englishmen and Scotsmen battling on the city walls. . . not much has changed.

One night some friends joined us at Becky's house for a few drinks before heading into town and we all got a little tipsy. We headed for a club in a really good party mood and the last thing on my mind was to go looking for trouble. In fact, with Becky in tow, I went out of my way to avoid getting into scraps but, if it couldn't be ignored or avoided, the one thing I wouldn't do was back away. It got dealt with the only way I knew how.

This was the time that I was bang into weights and steroids. The trouble is that, once you get really into the gear, you have to take a cocktail of them. It's a very misunderstood culture and quite an exact science. One steroid demands something else to counteract its side effects. What isn't in doubt is that steroid abuse can go very badly wrong and all too often does.

Note that I used the term 'abuse'. I'm not condoning their use, neither am I promoting it, but I will not condemn 'users' because, having done it myself, that would be hypocritical.

Abusers – well, they're on a slippery slope to serious health issues and, in the last few years, like tattoos, it's become an epidemic. Christ, every other kid I see in the gym or just walking around town is juiced up. Why? Because the actors they admire in films or celebs they see in magazines are all ripped and inked. The thing is that most of the black-market gear these guys are using is fake shit. They could be putting anything into their bodies. It's really fuckin' frightening. My advice to these boys is build real muscle; natural muscle. Don't risk your health like I did just whacking anything into your body because you want to look good on the beach.

All that said, as a result of my *use* of steroids, one of the drugs I was regularly taking was testosterone. Imagine: I was a big, active lad anyway and at an age when my natural testosterone levels were reaching their peak. Yet there was I juicing up on even more of the stuff. Test, as it is known, has side effects of its own, which generally manifest as acne – and aggression.

Think about it. When do boys turn from being little angels or imps into spotty, brooding grumps full of attitude and anger? Answer: during puberty, when their bodies are growing and changing and producing more and more testosterone. So juiced up and popped up to the eyeballs, we arrived at XS, a night club in the city. We hadn't been in there long when I caught the attention of a lad – let's just call him James Doe. James was well known around the city and feared by some, having accrued an inflated rep on account of being a bit of a head case and a nasty bastard. The chances are that he was whizzed up or on something else – who knows? For no apparent reason, he locked onto me.

It began with the old 'what you lookin' at? ' routine. You know the sort of thing: head cocked to one side and staring over to see who would be first to break eye contact. Backed up by his mates and with me trying to resist just dropping the tosspot, he obviously felt he had the upper hand. That's another mistake some handy lads and wannabes often make with me. They take my easy-going nature and reluctance to get into gear immediately as doubt or fear when it's more a case of, 'For fuck's sake, not another, not here, not now, not again.' I think that was what James was reading into the situation. That, or whatever he was on, had him convinced that he had what it took. Nowhere near enough was the truth of the matter.

Next thing they're all sharing knowing looks. His mates started egging him on; the kind of stuff you get from groups of half-cut arseholes who get off on ruining someone else's night. It started with nods in my direction, little nudges and his minions geeing James up to do the business. He was loving it, puffing himself up, acting the big man and really pushing his luck. Unfortunately for him, it had undertones of those bad times when Jamie and his gang used to bait me. That dragged up those old feelings of hatred into my guts. This lot had definitely targeted the wrong gadgey that night.

Their attentions finally got me revved up for action. Even Becky's soothing words and suggestion that I just ignore them weren't enough to calm me down. I instinctively knew that this was going to end in a fight and, if you recall my dad's sage advice from an earlier chapter, you'll know that I wasn't going to wait for them to make the first move: 'If someone has an imaginary problem with you, son, give them a real one.'

My patience finally ran out and, with it, James's luck. I steamed over to him and smacked the twat right in the jaw with an absolute corker of a right hook. One punch, *boom!* It sent him sprawling and scattered his mates, who, to a man, shit out. Typical! They were proper 'up for it' until that moment. No doubt had James, by some miracle, managed to drop me, they would have been right into me with their feet. With their 'scary-psycho' leader spread-eagled on the deck, all of a sudden not one of his grinning, gurning posse wanted any trouble – big surprise. Gutless worms.

After that they all pissed off, taking their still groggy ringleader with them. Before long, a guy I'd never met before sidled over to me, acting all pally. Now at this time, I hadn't got into recreational drugs of any kind but my new best mate slyly produced some Es and offered them to me at a special mates' rate. For a second or two I was gobsmacked, then smacked the drug-pushing c**t in the gob and knocked him out as well. Trip out on that, you twat! *Shit!* That shot hurt, though. I looked at my fist and saw why: one of his teeth had become lodged in my knuckle. I bear the scar to this day.

What I should have done after zeroing the drug dealer was go to the hospital but I didn't. The staff might have called the bizzies. Let's face it: a human tooth lodged in a knuckle is as good as a signed confession to ABH. I know not all cops are Sherlocks but all they'd have to do is check out my haunts. They'd find the clown with a big fat trout pout and bloody gap in his gob, then match it up to the tooth from my hand. As soon as the local cops heard the name Heggie, they'd have come looking. Who needs that?

We Heggies have provided work for dental practices and maxillofacial specialists since the early 1970s, thanks to Deccas Snr and Jnr. I bet we've swelled their pension pots over the years. Maybe we missed an opportunity there and should have been on a retainer. Anyway, instead of getting it treated, and with the body count rising at the night club, I took Becky home. I got the tooth out, washed the wound and went to bed.

The next morning I woke up with blood everywhere. My hand was like an inflated rubber glove and the puss that was filling it was creeping up my arm. This was serious but Becky, God bless her, helped me drain it and cleaned up the wound brilliantly. She was a really lovely, considerate, kind-hearted lass. Probably still is, 'cause I doubt a girl like her would ever change.

At the time, I didn't realise what I had. But after some time passed, being a stupid young bloke with a wandering eye, I cheated on her. I was young, well knocked together, and working on the doors. Temptation was on parade every weekend, and I succumbed.

When Becky found out, that was it. She finished with me. To this day, above all the other shit that has happened, it is the greatest regret of my life. If I could turn the clock back and ignore that temptress, I'd like to think – even dream sometimes – that I'd still be with Becky. So I'm going to take this opportunity to apologise to her. I betrayed her trust and hurt her. She definitely did not deserve to be treated that way. It was disrespectful; inexcusable. If it's any consolation, Becky, it's been a source of pain and regret for me ever since. I have deliberately not used her surname so as not to cause her any embarrassment. Becky may never have given another thought in years to that big, daft lad she once loved but, hopefully, if she has, and if she is reading this book, she will realise I am sincere. After all this time, she might find it in her heart to forgive me.

The break-up with Becky pushed me towards the edge and I wasn't very good company for a while. Then one night, I was paired up on the door at XS with a lad I hadn't worked with before. When it quietened down a bit, he produced a small bag of Charlie. He told me that he'd patted down a punter and taken his drugs off him. No carrying, no selling, no using on the premises – it was a house rule. What wasn't in the rules was taking it yourself but he did and offered me some. I was in a proper mood and thought, 'Fuck it. Why the hell not?'

By then, with Becky long gone, I'd lost my inhibitions towards drugs. I had already dabbled in Es and dropped speed, as well as still taking steroids. Not only that, I'd sniffed clouds of solvents as a kid and survived that. What harm was a line of coke going to do? Loads, as it happened.

That night on the door was my first hit of cocaine. For eight years thereafter I was hooked on the fuckin' stuff. I bought, begged or nicked it from punters, just like my mate had shown me that first time. It became a doddle to spot the ones using Charlie. As soon as they'd paid the cashier, we'd pull them, frisk them and confiscate their wraps or bags. Once the coast was clear, we'd pop into the bogs and snort it ourselves. Naughty but nice. Too nice! I couldn't get enough. It completely took over my life.

Before long, those drug dealers I'd once hated and avoided became friends. Not real friends but friends by mutual convenience. I needed their product; they needed a big, handy lad who could collect outstanding debts. Addiction strips away any scruples you might have and, eventually, all of your principles. I was leaning on other addicts to get money off them for the dealers and doing things that now leave me feeling deeply ashamed. I'd become something I deplore: a bully.

Of course, that wasn't how I saw it at the time. To use that old cliché, it wasn't personal, it was just business; supply and demand. The customer had taken the product on tick and payment was due. If they defaulted on that payment, Decca would come knocking on the door or tap them on the shoulder in a pub or corner them in the bogs. Some of them were just taking the piss and never had any intention of coughing up the readies. They deserved the final reminder they got but too many were desperate and pathetic addicts with a habit they couldn't afford or kick. Then one day I overstepped the mark. I'd been after a particular lad for a while, chasing him down over £800. By the time I caught him in, never mind the dealer, I was pissed off with him. He'd had his warnings and it was time for a hard lesson. I gave him a bit of roughhousing.

What had I become? Yet that lad didn't grass me up, even with his mother in his ear. I'd have done some decent time for that but that poor guy took his punishment without complaint. You cannot do that sort of work and have a conscience and that was a wake-up call for mine. Believe it or not, it was also a wake-up for him as well. He got clean after that house call and we eventually became friends. I even went to his mother and begged for her forgiveness. God Bless her, she gave it and to this day will always stop for a craic when we meet.

I still live with the anger, anguish, mental torment and the threat of depression and it's all down to the drug abuse of my past. I also think the anxiety I lived with for several years thanks to Jamie and his friends played their part. However, my real problems didn't really begin until I started messing about with solvents before moving on to cocaine and other so-called recreational drugs.

Now I am thirty-two years old. I am proud to say that I haven't drunk alcohol or touched any of that shit in over three years. People look at me and see a strapping, healthy young man who is in great shape but all they see is what's on the outside. My mind is damaged for life. No psychiatrist will sort my head out and I've never used anti-depressants. As a result, that Black Dog slips its leash from time to time, tracks me down and digs me out.

Living with the side-effects of my drug-taking years gets me angry. Sometimes it leaves me feeling like some crazy masochist. Why did I do this to myself? What the hell was I thinking? I inflicted the mental torture I now live with, no one else. That is why I never ask for, or expect, pity or sympathy. What I do is tell other kids not to make the same mistakes. Stay away from drugs, keep away from solvents and just remember this: if you do mess with them, you will fall into a trap from which few escape.

I don't know of a single addict who, when they started to take them, didn't think that they could handle using drugs. Like me, they all said to themselves, 'I'll just enjoy the ride for a while and then jack it in as soon as it causes me any problems.' Easier said than done. Stimulants might make you feel on top of the world while you're under their influence but a few short years down the line, maybe sooner, and they will show their true colours.

It might begin like it did with me, sniffing glue or getting messy on stolen cans of lager or cheap cider bought with the money you've nicked off members of your family. You've only just got into it and already you're acting like scum! I'm not making excuses but, in my defence, getting wasted on glue and solvents, as well getting pissed on cheap cider, was a way of escaping the bullying. It didn't stop it happening but it stopped it from hurting. When wrecked, I neither cared what they did nor felt a thing. It took away the pain and the embarrassment. That's the kind of place bullying can take a kid. Be mindful of that if you ever suspect it's happening to someone you care about – to anyone for that matter.

What I can guarantee you if you take the drug route is this: you'll slowly be dragged down into a pitiful existence that revolves around 'the fix', 'the hit' and nothing else, reduced to doing whatever it takes to fund your habit. No self-respect, nor respect for anyone else, no dignity, no morals. Thankfully, I woke from that particular nightmare before I was reduced to any of that but only because I damn near killed myself with an overdose. Others aren't so lucky. What I advise people now is to dig out a local addict from their street shelter or flea-pit of a doss house, or go to any drug-counselling group. I don't know of anyone who has met one person whose life has been improved by the use of drugs or alcohol. I'm telling you, that person doesn't exist.

Lecture over – for now. Back to the craic. No, not crack cocaine! It's Cumbrian or Gaelic for chat, gossip – in this case, my story.

CHAPTER SIX

COPS AND BOTHER

I got a bit ahead of myself in chapter five so I'm going to take us back to the days that I worked on the security circuit. To be honest, when I was a doorman, I rarely had or got into much trouble. The local cops knew the score and needed us more than we needed them. It's true. Good door staff can calm or stop a situation long before it escalates and spills into the streets.

Despite being on the wrong end of a few accusations, I don't have a downer on the police. Where the hell would we be without them? However, that uniform is only as good as the man or woman wearing it and a few too many of them seem to think that it is all that is needed to quieten a situation down – a few too many more also think it's an Iron-Man outfit. Wrong!

Occasionally you'd get the job's-worth 'Robo-plod' turn up at the door who has believed the first thing he was told without question. You know the sort of scenario. They just leap to the conclusion that the big bully on the door picked on the little guy who has gone bitching to them with a complaint. Nine times out of ten they'd be responding to some whinging twat who had – *maybe* – been given a bit of a slap for being a dickhead or had started some trouble that we had quickly pounced on. Often as not, after I'd given my side of the story, the cops would impart a little cautionary but obvious advice and go away happy. Occasionally it got a little more heated.

If any young coppers who've just got into the job are reading this, listen to me. The one with the black eye or fat lip might well be the loser but it doesn't mean he's the innocent party. Don't believe the first thing you are told. Listen to both sides of the argument and make a balanced decision. I've lost count of the number of horrible little c**ts I've kicked out of the clubs and pubs for kicking off or picking fights, who then went on to complain that they have been assaulted: often as not by the door staff whose job it is to escort them off the premises.

Fortunately for me, I was good at talking to people. I rarely had to resort to the heavy stuff but things had begun to get proper dodgy. We were turning up nearly as many knives and other weapons as we were drugs and fake IDs. As a result, even I had started carrying a blade. *I know!* Christ, if the boss had found out, he would have sacked my arse on the spot. Now, as I look back on those times, I realise how crazy that was but it's a mad world, and getting worse if you ask me. At the time, though, it kind of made sense and that's the thing when you're using Charlie: the worst idea in the world can seem like the best you've ever had.

Add to that the fact that I was a young, juiced-up mass of raging testosterone and too stupid to recognise that. I had got it into my head that, if something kicked off and I was outnumbered, and with so many boys carrying blades, I would meet like with like. Paranoia had begun to kick in – another side effect of coke addiction. I was hitting the stuff real hard and, although it kept me on my toes, it was really fucking up my head but I just couldn't see it. A bouncer with a blade – I ask you: how messed up is that? All it would have taken is for some arsehole to flick the wrong switch and I might have ended up doing life.

I can remember being in The Walkabout, an Australian Bar down Botchergate, on the east side of Carlisle, with two or three mates having a couple of beers on top of a few lines of Charlie. I wasn't working or tooled up but, owing to the job and the coke, I was wired and my radar was constantly scanning for trouble. A bunch of rowdy Leeds United fans came in. Then the football chants started. They were trying to impress everyone, coming across like members of the notorious Inter-City Firm hooligans but were probably just wannabes. Whatever, they were up for a bit of action.

My hackles rose the minute they entered. Once they started giving it loads of gob and acting like the owned the place, a ruck was definitely on the cards. We get it all the time in Carlisle from visiting football fans, especially the hooligan elements from bigger cities. I could see one or two punters were getting a bit nervous but not me – I was getting revved up. To be honest, by then, my head was a shed. I couldn't predict what I might do from one minute to the next and neither could anyone else. Drink, speed and Charlie had me behaving like a total maniac at times.

Anyway, these idiots were getting on my tits. I just looked at my mates and said, 'Are we having some?' They shrugged, nodded and, as one, we got stuck right into them. I knocked two out and the lads levelled a couple of others. Leeds was losing big-style to Carlisle but somebody called the cops and I found myself in the cells. The worst part about it was that I didn't give a fuck. I'd gone from drug-free, happy-go-lucky, loved-up lump to a steroid-fuelled, coke-headed psycho in the space of a couple of years.

Even getting sent to prison didn't calm me down. Oh yeah – been there, done that. It began with my mate Mike's stag do to Blackpool. Sixteen of us went into Carlisle at ten in the morning for a few beers at The Walkabout before jumping on a train to Blackpool, with bags of carry-outs, of course. We arrived in the candy-floss capital in fine fettle. Of course, a bunch of noisy drunken young guys always attracts the attention of other gangs of pissed-up likely lads – in our case, a coachload from Darlington.

This time I can honestly say that we didn't start anything but neither did we back off when they did. I bumped into one of them as I was trying to get to the bar. He got a bit stroppy and said I'd spilled his drink. Even though he was still holding what looked like a full pint to me, I apologised and went to leave but he grabbed my arm and told me to buy him another.

In such situations, it pays not to take your eye off the guy with the glass or you might find yourself picking it out of your face but still, in my 20-20 vision, I could see a few of his mates squaring off. Working the doors and being a lad who was used to a bit of a ruck, I could read the signs and knew what was coming next. We were outnumbered. The Darlington crew fancied the odds. This was a hair-trigger moment and he was about to pull it, so I got the first shot in; three rapid shots, to be precise. If I hadn't caused him to spill his beer before, he showered his mates with it that time. Next thing you know, everyone's into gear.

The battle spilled out of the pub into the street and this huge, six-foot-plus steroid monster homed in on me. I reckon he must have been at least twenty stone but I didn't give a shit. I ripped into him with a salvo of my best shots, which had him huffing, puffing and staggering all over the place. I could see the look of panic on his face as I powered into him. He might have been a really big lad but he moved with the speed of a glacier and I had him beat when someone else grabbed my arm as I drew back to finish him off.

Without looking around, because I still had the big lad to deal with, I just took a quick step back to put whoever it was off balance, then lashed out to shake him off, catching him right in the face with my forearm. He screamed with pain and shouted, 'Bastard! You're fuckin' nicked!' It was only then that I realised he'd clipped a handcuff onto my wrist as he grabbed me and that it had caught him. Bollocks! It was a copper and, in no time, reinforcements arrived.

I was cuffed and bundled into the back of a van. Being arrested wasn't the worst of it. When they got me back to the nick and into a cell, about half a dozen of the twats piled in and knocked lumps out of me. What a fuckin' hiding I got.

'Think you're a tough guy, do yer?' one of them grunted as he rattled my ribcage and his mates put their elbows, feet and knees into me.

'Tougher than you cowardly bastards,' I thought but I didn't say so. I'd like to have seen any of them take me on one-on-one. The funny thing was that they were all puffing and blowing when they left the cell. Two minutes and out of steam! I laughed at them just to show I was stronger than all of them put together. What an unfit shower of shit they were. The thin blue line? Yellow ones more like, right down their spines.

I was kept in overnight, charged the following morning with affray and police assault and sent straight into the Magistrates' Court. So there I was, looking like Quasimodo's uglier kid brother. The lying bastards obviously told the prosecutor, who in turn told the bench, that all of my bruises and other injuries were a result of the mass brawl in which I'd been involved.

'Yer having a laugh?' I said. 'The fuckin' coppers that arrested me did all this. Those arseholes from Darlington never landed one good shot.'

Guilty, fined, bound over, put on a curfew and tagged. There's justice for you. Fair enough, I was well out of order and in the thick of a right old tear-up, and I suppose I did smack the arresting officer across the chops – but not intentionally. I thought it was one of the big lad's mates giving him a hand because I had him beat. What they just didn't want to hear was that I'd been given a proper going over, while cuffed, by half a dozen coppers or so. That was bang out of order, not to mention a blatant case of ABH.

If you've never been tagged, trust me: those ankle bracelets are uncomfortable bits of kit and I think they'd put mine on a bit too tight. After a short while, I got so pissed off with it that I cut it off with a pair of scissors. That was in breach of the conditions of my release. Within hours I was locked up and in Carlisle's police cells. There was a brief court hearing, at which no fucker was listening to a word I said, and I was whisked back to the cells. Next thing you know, I've got one-way ticket to HMP Durham for three months.

I arrived there in a pretty bad shape, having gone cold turkey from the Charlie in a bid to break my addiction and knowing I'd struggle to get my hands on any behind the door anyway. Like most nicks, Durham is full of people with, or looking to build, a reputation so, despite not being fighting fit, I had to stay alert. They didn't scare me but you don't have to do a thing to get jumped inside. I was fully expecting one of them to take a pop at the first opportunity.

Cumbrians often get a bit of a hard time in Durham, especially ones that look a bit handy. That's because the Geordies and Mackems that dominate the prison's population think of it as home turf. There's some real tasty bastards among them. You've got petty thieves living alongside armed robbers, hardcore gangsters and convicted murderers. Anyone that gets banged up from our side of the Pennines is just looked upon as a numpty sheep shagger who needs to be kept in place. That's why a lad from Carlisle has to watch his back.

E-Wing at Durham is the induction wing and, as new arrivals, activities are really restricted. It's a minging spot full of smack-heads and bag-heads. You can't even open the cell window there and so it gets really claustrophobic when you're banged up for twenty-three hours out of twenty-four. It stinks too, what with two of you sharing a small space with one bog! Prison – a soft option these days, is it? Try it. I sure as hell never want to go back.

I might have been off the coke and feeling like shit but my body still coursed with steroids. I was itching to get to the prison gym but couldn't. Access to the gym is restricted to inmates who have been allocated to a residential wing, so I filled out the form to get transferred onto D-wing.

On the upside, D-wing was reserved for inmates who demonstrate good behaviour. However, the ground floor was also where they held the beasts and nonces. I suppose their reasoning was that well-behaved prisoners, who just want to get their bird done and dusted without any hassle, won't risk a longer spell by bashing nonces. Makes sense, I suppose, but sharing a wing with paedophiles, beasts, pervs and rapists is not where any straight con wants to be. Thank fuck I was sent up to the top landing, two floors above the sick bastards.

My first pad-mate was a smack-head. Let's call him Leo. He was all right but, like most addicts, a fidgety, nervous fucker. It's a real pain sharing a confined space with a smack-head who's pacing and twitching like a schizoid weasel. When his meds came, he showed me a trick you could do with Subutex (Sub). Sub is a drug they issue to the heroin addicts. It prevents the effects of withdrawal. What you do is grind it into a powder and snort the stuff. Not the best buzz ever but better than nowt for a coke fiend with only four walls, daytime TV and a manic smack-head to break the boredom.

Leo got moved and I next found myself padded up with a Newcastle lad I'll call Bobby, who turned out to be a top bloke. Bobby was your typical Geordie wide-boy but happy to keep a low profile. His priority was to get his bird done without any fuss and get home ASAP. He was a good laugh too. We would pass the time playing blackjack all day long for our canteen money. I cannot get my head around how habitual jailbirds and lifers hack being behind the door for years on end. After a few days, I was bored to tears and began to make scratch marks on the bottom of my bed for each one I'd spent there. All too soon for me, not him, Geordie Bobby got his release and his replacement arrived the same day.

He wandered in with a sickly smile on his pasty chops and his bits and pieces cradled in his arms. As soon as I saw his face, I knew what it was – a nonce. He chatted away like I was an old mate as he sorted his shit out and settled down. This dirty bastard was so open about why he was inside that I think he thought he was sharing with a fellow beast. I'm not gonna tell you because thinking about it still makes me sick to my stomach. Within minutes of that piece of shit parking his arse on his bunk, I was fighting myself not to smash the depraved fucker to a pulp. Ten minutes tops he'd been there when I was on the buzzer and banging the door.

When the screw came to the hatch, I told him, 'Get this c**t out of here before I smash him to bits.'

That particular screw, Mr Wilson, was all right. I got on really well with him but not all of them. Some of them were proper arseholes who strutted about the place on a power trip. I'd love to have got one or two of them in the ring or pit to find out whether they could walk the walk as good as they talked the talk. Mr Wilson, though, he was sound as a pound and got it sorted pronto. Next thing you know, the nonce was gone and I never saw him again but I heard that he got the shit hammered right out of him in shower room. I'd be happy to see the bastard hang.

Behind the door, the shower room was where most scores were settled. It's the only place where the screws aren't looking over your shoulder. I suppose they don't want to be tarred with the nonce brush by being accused of perving. As it was, during my time in there, despite catching the eye of a few of the prison's hard-cases, I only had one fairly minor bit of aggravation.

There was this cocky twat from Sunderland who worked in the kitchens and thought he was Jack-the-fuckin'-lad. One day, as my turn came around, he gave me less food than everybody else. I don't mean he skimped on a bit of mash or gave me a few less peas; I mean he made it obvious that that was all I was getting. I don't know why. We'd had no ag beforehand. So I told him I wanted some more scran. He just sniggered and ignored me. Big mistake.

I caught up with the Mackem bastard in the showers. A quick scan for screws, all clear and *crunch*! I stuck the nut on him. He went down but wasn't out. I waited for him to get back onto his feet. When he did, he came up swinging but missed and I banged the bastard clean out. Unlike me, he didn't ask for more of what I was dishing out. Pity – I'd have happily obliged.

A screw spotted me coming out of the showers and him laid out on the deck but didn't put me on report. Something must have been said though because I missed out on the earliest release date that was available under the terms of my sentence. Oh well. Carlisle 1–Sunderland 0 and I got my fair share come feeding time.

After Leo moved on, I quickly identified a source and secured a fairly regular supply of Sub, which meant I could do a few little lines now and again and sometimes drop Tramadol. It's a painkiller that contains morphine and that, together with the Sub, helped to get me through my short stretch in a reasonably mellow frame of mind but my comfy existence was almost blown by my next cell-mate. As I've done with the others, I'll change his name to Hammed.

I swear that I can get on with anyone provided they meet me halfway. So it didn't matter to me who I was sharing with. But I could tell from the moment he entered the cell that it bothered Hammed that he was being made to share with me. During his short stay, he proved to be the rudest bloke I was padded up with. Even the nonce, for the very short time he was with me, wasn't rude but he was a nonce and fuckin' proud of it, to hear him talk. I don't care how good his manners were, I would have had to smash him to pieces if they had let him stay.

This guy was proper up himself, though. Hammed looked down his nose at me; called me ignorant because of the stuff I read and watched on TV and said I was dirty because I used the loo more than he did and wiped my arse with paper. This from a fella who used his bare hand when he had a shite, then washed it in the sink we shared. I used to waste my own soap washing the sink before I'd wash my hands and face in it. But that wasn't the worst of sharing with Hammed. He objected to the daytime telly I would watch. It's not as if we were spoiled for choice when it came to in-cell entertainment. Telly, cards, snorting Sub and reading – that's your lot.

Of course, the whinging arse-wipe wanted to watch anything but what I wanted to and complained to the screws that I was being racist and bullying him when he didn't get his own way. One of us had to go or I would never have qualified for early release and go he did. Bobby, if you're reading this mate: for that short time we were banged up together, you were a diamond and I hope you're still free and happy, my friend. Even Leo wasn't bad for a skanky smack-head but those other two!

My release eventually came halfway through my sentence,

on account of my good behaviour. The screw who'd seen me leaving the showers must have just worded someone but not pressed for an extension. The Mackem from the canteen hadn't said anything about me knocking him out, for two reasons, I suspect. First, he was doing a longer stretch and had his own rep to consider. Second, he'd have been labelled a grass; loathed on the outside but something that could, in extreme cases, result in a death sentence behind the door.

After my release, I kept my head down until my licence was spent. I got back to working the doors and doing Charlie like there was no tomorrow. Free and easy and with a night off work, I went down the town and made my way to XS. While I was there, I bumped into a girl I knew called Dawn. She used the same gym as me and we used to have a laugh, flirt a bit, but never anything more. We'd exchange hellos and smiles around the place but it never crossed my mind to make a move on her. I thought of Dawn as a mate, nothing more.

As I was heading down to the toilets, we met on the stairs and, for no reason at all, I playfully slapped her arse. It was a liberty, granted; a stupid, spontaneous thing to do and, in retrospect, disrespectful even but, at the time, she didn't react in a way that suggested I'd been out of order. The rest of the night passed by without incident and I never thought anything more about it until closing time. Then I had a lot to think about. The police were waiting for me and arrested me for indecent assault. In a reckless moment and out of an ill-considered sense of fun, I had cheekily slapped what I thought was a mate's arse and ended up in court.

When asked how I pleaded, I held my hands up and said, 'Yeah, sorry your worships but I did slap her on the arse.' That was the truth and it cost me a £300 fine. Far worse than the money was a four-year ban from working the doors. God's truth, that sentence was way more devastating than the three months banged up for breaking my curfew. The local press went to town on me. They made me sound like a beast. The headline ran something like: DOORMAN FINED FOR FONDLING WOMAN IN NIGHT CLUB.

That incident and the press's version of events tainted my life and sent me spiralling out of control. Like addicts do, I tried to soothe the anger, embarrassment and genuine feelings of injustice by taking shed-loads of coke. All that did was turn me into a brooding monster who even some of my friends avoided. Or was it that they believed I was a sex pest? Do you see what a thing like that does to your head? Were they scared 'cause I'd become unpredictable and aggressive? Or were they embarrassed to be seen with me? I couldn't tell you. I can tell you this, though: I carry that verdict like a ton weight. Trust me: ever since, around lasses, I've kept my hands to myself until there is absolutely no doubt that they want my attentions.

Unemployed and unemployable, the slide had begun into coked-up oblivion. I was hanging out with a lad called Carl a lot at that time and we'd gone to a party. We had the company of a couple of ladies and enough coke to keep us happy all night. Sounds good, eh? But this was a very bad time in my life. I kept slipping into deep depression and relying on coke to lift me again. The trouble was that coke was the root of the problem, not the solution!

As it was, I ended up getting completely off my face. I pulled a machete off the wall and, for no reason, started swinging it at the others. Thinking about it, who the fuck keeps a machete hanging on the wall in the first place? A great big, fuck-off jungle knife for an ornament. It makes no sense, does it? But that was the kind of company I was keeping by then. Drug-induced paranoia saw me come very close to killing someone.

The next day I checked myself into the Carlton Clinic – a place that mainly caters for people with mental-health problems. I was so messed up back then that much of my twenties is a blur, purely on account of either being shit-faced or scoped out on coke or other drugs, or a cocktail of them all.

So there I was cabbaged out in a clinic with an unlicensed fight just four days away. It will come as no surprise to read that I lost on points against a guy called Stuart Oscar Irwin, who is well known on the circuit. Oscar, as he prefers to be known, is a big hitter and as hard as nails but a cracking lad. That, for me, is one of the great joys of my sport. I can step into a ring or pit and take on another hard bloke I've never met before. Come the end of the fight, win or lose, I have made a new friend. It's a friendship based on mutual respect.

Losing that first fight against Oscar was another hard lesson. I wasn't ring ready, hadn't prepared and was still suffering the effects of drying out from that last mad binge. I shouldn't have been anywhere near a boxing ring. Mine were not the actions of a fighter who was taking his boxing seriously. Worse still, I was being disrespectful to the people I was booked to fight and the sport I love. That is inexcusable. So to all of them I also send out a belated apology. Decca was being a dickhead and needed to sort himself the fuck out.

Breaking free from a cycle of addiction is easier said than done. That fight at least gave me a wake-up call. Sadly, all it took was for that Black Dog to rear its ugly head and I'd weaken and reach for the nose candy. Not anymore. I like to keep my wits about me at all time these days as sometimes a young gun will come along wanting a pop at trying to take my titles. The best way to combat that is to stay fighting fit and in the best shape I can twenty four/seven.

These days, the highs come in the shape of a worthy opponent or preparing for such an encounter. The buzz these days comes from pummelling a heavy bag or a going on a good run, pumping iron or flipping tractor tyres with Macca. The lows are as they always were but are less frequent and don't linger as long.

CHAPTER SEVEN

OSCAR NIGHTS AND OTHER FIGHTS

During the early days of my fighting career on the unlicensed boxing circuit, I had two classic fights with Stuart Oscar Irwin. By classic, I don't mean they were in the best pugilistic traditions of the game or particularly bouts of the highest quality but they were good value for money; unrelenting and hard fought. Two very different but evenly matched fighters and neither of us gave or expected quarter.

I tend to adopt a half-crouch stance and press forward with a pile-driver jab but can also catch opponents out with sharp counter-punching, whereas Oscar is a very mobile and tricky switch-hitter. When executed skilfully, it's a great technique for picking up points and Oscar is good.

Oscar weighed in at around fifteen stone but he could bang away like a super-heavyweight. He was there among the hardest hitters I have ever faced. Back then, I was not the dedicated athlete I am today. I was a bulky, steroid-fuelled coke-head who also took Valium on a fairly regular basis and drank Scotch like a bus-load of Jocks at a free bar.

Needless to say, Oscar beat me both times. I'd be willing to bet, though, that on more than one occasion he has asked himself the question: 'How come I couldn't I knock Decca out?'

Believe me: he tried. That lad hit me with everything he had. I must admit, I've often wondered how *he* stayed on his feet. I might not have been in the sort of nick I am now when I step into the ring but I never lacked strength and could still punch most fellas' lights out but not Oscar's.

For that first fight in Workington, I'd done three lines of Charlie before I climbed into the ring. On top of that, I weighed in at a shamefully unfit nineteen stone. A four-stone advantage is great if you have the stamina to carry you through all the rounds but a huge burden if you haven't. In the stamina department, I was definitely lacking.

Nevertheless, brute power alone saw me dominate the first round. I had him against the ropes, delivering some heavy shots to his head, face and body, but he soaked them all up. Before the bell went for the end of the round, it was dawning on me that, if I didn't put him away quick, I was going to lose. I tried but would he go down? Would he hell.

In the second round I again started strong but, in no time, was feeling the effects of lactic acid kicking in, as first my arms knotted up, quickly followed by my legs. It's a horrible feeling, as any athlete will tell you. There is absolutely nothing you can do about it as your muscles burn, then tighten and seize up altogether. Soon I was plodding around the ring like I was wading through treacle as he bobbed and dipped and side-stepped my attempts to corner him.

Oscar sensed I was in trouble and kicked up a gear. He began to dominate the round, catching me with three massive, poorly guarded shots that put me on the ropes. He followed them up with four vicious hooks, left-right-left-right, and down I went. No doubt he will claim a knockdown and fair enough, technically it was, but I seem to recall simply falling because my body had seized up and my legs had virtually stopped working. Cramped, spent and exhausted, I somehow rallied, stood before the count ended and got stuck back in until the end of the round.

By the time they called 'seconds out' for the third round, I'd caught my breath and was back on my toes. I started pressing forward again and caught him with two great shots. He staggered but, fair play to him, rode them like a true pro. Once again I slowed down and became drained of power and he finally pinched the fight on points. Taking nothing away from Oscar (he's a brave, game and canny fighter with a punch that few people could handle) but that second-round fall, knockdown, call it what you want, cost me the fight.

A rematch was set up and took place six months after I got out of jail following my three-month sentence for cutting off my ankle tag. By that time, my life was dominated by coke and the steroids. Although I was gaining mass, there was no focus to anything I was doing; no regime, no plan or ultimate goal. Just the crazy coke-addled delusion that I was the next Lenny McLean or something and that everything would work out just fine.

All I cared about was getting enough gear into me to make myself strong and massive, getting pissed and getting enough Charlie to make my shit, pointless existence seem great. Meanwhile, my fitness level had dropped off the scale and my head was completely fucked up. Days drifted by in a daze or depressions as deep as a sinkhole. It was idiotic, especially with the Oscar rematch at Carlisle's Hilltop Hotel literally around the corner.

The Hilltop is just down the road from our estate and was the home of unlicensed boxing in Carlisle. I had quite a few scraps there, including my first ever, that win over Mickey German. I had a rematch with him as well in Preston that he won on points. Same prep as with Oscar, you see: kidding myself that my size, strength and natural power would overcome quality fighters like Mickey and Oscar. What a clown I'd turned into; I should have been in a Big Top, not a boxing ring. One all – honours even Mickey; God bless you, a real gentleman and legend in the unlicensed game.

Oscar, in complete contrast to me, was taking his fighting very seriously. He was delivering KO after KO fight after fight but none of them had my chin. Our second fight saw me start strong again but, as with the first, my lack of fitness let me down. In the first round I cracked him with a proper solid right hand. Oscar stumbled but stayed upright and leaned back against the ropes. Lovely! I had him pinned and poured it on but the bell went and he was off the hook.

After putting everything into that furious first round, my face was as red as a baboon's arse and I was blowing like a whale with asthma. Throwing nineteen stone of muscle around a ring when you're totally wired on Charlie and haven't done any roadwork or cardio soon empties the tank. Ask Oscar if you ever meet him. He will tell you how he knocked me from pillar to post for the next two rounds and never once put me down.

At the end of the fight I think everyone, including him, was shocked that I could still walk, let alone climb out of the ring. He was knackered too because he'd used every weapon in his arsenal – clubbing hooks, left and right, piston-like jabs and vicious uppercuts – but he could not put me away. The ref just left him to go about his work. That's unlicensed boxing for you. Yes, he'd bob in for a quick look when Oscar stepped back for a breather but then he'd wave him on and Oscar would unload another punishing series of combinations.

He threw everything but the kitchen sink at me but I have a jaw like reinforced steel. Nobody knocks me out – ever! That's why I've been so successful on the BKB circuit. At least, once I'd got my nose out of the candy and binned the steroids, shed the excess weight and cut the drink out of my life. Yeah, success finally came after I'd got my head out of my arse. My ability to take a punch and keep throwing them when my opponents are spent has taken me to the top. That's where I plan to stay. Getting there, however, has been a brutal climb.

Taking nothing away from the men I've fought on the unlicensed circuit, the bareknuckle game takes you to another level of fear and pain. There's no pinching a win on points either. You just pound away until one or the other falls or folds or the ref decides he's seen enough. Ambulances are occasionally called after a bout but nobody wants to see a hearse roll up to take the loser away. Some sadistic psychos might but very few of the fighters. We're there for pride and the purse, not to kill each other.

I'm not saying that my gloved opponents couldn't hack it; some have had a bash and decided it wasn't for them. I'm pretty sure some others would also fare really well should they gave it a try. It's either in you as a fighter or it isn't to take that step outside your comfort zone and remove those gloves.

Every boxer knows that, once the gloves are off, it ups the ante on the injury stakes.

The baseline in BKB is: if it doesn't hurt, you're not trying. For a start you're risking your hands every time you throw a punch. The human skull is a very hard object. Miscue a knockout shot and catch them on the top of the head as they duck and something's gotta give. What use is a boxer with broken hands?

Lenny McLean was always dislocating his knuckles and breaking bones in his hands during fights but pain never stopped that crazy bastard. Being the kind of fighting animal he was, he ignored the pain until his opponent was down and out. Afterwards he would just get his hands fixed-up and was bang at it again as soon as they had healed. You can only reset bones so many times before they're no longer fit for purpose. I'd bet my next three purses that poor Lenny, God rest his soul, had he lived into old age, would have been crippled by arthritis in his hands before he reached sixty.

Then there's being on the receiving end. Bare knuckles can open up cuts far easier and more quickly than a gloved fist. Teeth get knocked out, gums split, jaws broken, cheekbones fractured and noses broken – but not mine. Check it out: not even a little bit bent. Eyebrows, ears and lips get split on a regular basis. Every fight has the potential to turn into a right old bloodbath. I fuckin' love it.

If you remember, I said that once I'd realised I could fight I didn't mind being hit. That's not bullshit. I get off on it 'cause it gives me something more than I had when I stepped into the pit or ring. Every blow turns over a cog in my system that ratchets up my adrenaline level and generates even more power and aggression. It's as if they're transferring their power to me and making me stronger. Of course, I always return it – with added interest.

The least impressive of my fights generally all have something in common. My opponent wasn't doing the business. If they box clever and tap away at me, I'll hit them hard. Should they land a hammer blow, I'll respond by trying to punch a hole clean through the fucker. I've never lost in a bareknuckle fight but I had two that were declared a draw. The verdict is something you just have to accept but I didn't agree with either of them.

They were tricky fights against two big, hard-men, who are very skilful fighters. Those were the cagey, tactical kind of bouts that I've just described. As a result, during both those fights we spent way too much time circling each other, probing for weaknesses, trying to prize open each other's defences. When all that's going on, I'm not feeding off their power or aggression as much. I prefer a proper toe-to-toe, 'blood-and-guts' style tear-up.

Yes, we got into gear but only in brief, violent exchanges and I don't care what result the ref declares, a fighter knows when he's dominating a fight and he knows when he has won. I can't speak for my two opponents or give you their take on the results but it doesn't sit easy with me. It doesn't matter what I think, it's there in black and white on my fight stats: won ten, drawn two – and that's that.

One of those guys, Stevan Miller was all over Facebook as far back as July 2015 declaring that we were in 'advanced talks' for a rematch. If so, it was news to me and my management team. I'll tell you about that fight later but Stevan has really gone down in my estimation by going public after a friendly private craic mate-to-mate. What was actually said, in a friendly phone call to give him a 'heads-up' about the book, was that I would be happy to fight him again but that he would have to talk to Macca.

At the time of writing, Stevan hasn't made any such approach but, weirdly, has declared that he'd go around Macca to talk to my dad about a rematch. If you're reading this, Stevan, listen up: my dad will never undermine Macca – they are the best of mates. Shouting about rematches on social media does not, in mine, or their books, constitute advanced talks. No, that's what's known as wishful thinking, mate. So! Patience Stevan: who knows what the future holds? But as I've said before, be careful what you wish for.

Despite the fact that I was a mess throughout my twenties, when drugs, drink and partying ruled my life, and despite not putting in the training or graft to keep myself fighting fit, I couldn't stay out of the ring. I took on lots of fighters. People such as Glaswegian heavyweight John 'Cruel Intentions' Stevens, who had forty-nine undefeated fights under his belt when we touched gloves. Well named is Cruel John because he's a real tough bastard in the best Glaswegian tradition; well capable of giving any fighter a proper hard time.

Every city has a dark underbelly that breeds hard-men. There are few places in the UK more notorious for producing gangsters, vicious street-fighters and quality boxers across just about every weight division than Scotland's second city of Glasgow. Even the infamous Kray twins of London's East End – no soft manor itself – used to recruit Weegie muscle for their particular brand of savagery.

Not wishing to take anything away from John but I was not in the best of shape when we fought. I look back at that fight on YouTube and think, 'You look like shit, Decca. What a mug.' John's a justifiably confident fighter because he's good, strong and can take a punch. He must have looked at me and thought, 'Piece of piss.' I was very tense but he was in control, even toying with me a little between exchanges.

With a lot more work and dedication I, too, might have boasted an undefeated record. As it was, I had to hit bottom before I realised it was 'lie down and be remembered as an also ran' or 'wake the fuck up and show the world the real Decca Heggie.'

John's one of those canny fighters that stays just out of reach, not offering much of a defence, arms down and leaning in to tempt you to take a pop at his jaw. Of course, that's why you're there, so you oblige. Then *boom*! With lightning speed he counters and gets around your guard. For a big fella, Cruel John is very fast and nimble. He throws accurate, thudding jabs and rips into you with vicious combinations.

We went six rounds. He took the win on points, with one judge scoring us even, but I'm not complaining. It was a hard fight, a well-earned win and a fair result. John 'Cruel Intentions' Stevens is a big man and a quality boxer who earned and still enjoys my respect. One of Glasgow's finest.

Another fighter I took on, this time at Walker in Newcastle, was a Geordie night-club doorman. A man with a tasty rep and massive punch to back it up: James 'Boom-Boom' Barnes. I put him on his arse in the first round after only eight seconds but he was straight back up and, after a standing count, got stuck in. The second round saw him come out with all guns blazing. Boom-Boom was swinging with real intent. He really got through with some sharp and clever combinations that I was having trouble countering.

He really poured it on for a spell and we punished each other in that round.

He landed several body-shuddering shots to my head, which I felt all the way down to my toes, as he tried to make up for that earlier knock-down. Rumours of his big-hitting ability weren't exaggerated. What a punch that guy's got! But it wasn't enough. As we probed, prodded and punished each other, James whispered, 'I wish you'd go down.'

No chance. But he did again in round three. I had the measure of him by then. A win was only a matter of – when? Round four, as it happened. By a knockout! Boom-Boom is one seriously tough Geordie. I bet they don't have too much bother when he's on the door.

They don't come much more experienced than Mark Greener. A forty-year-old veteran of two hundred fights when we met at the 'War in Workington' for the Cumbria heavyweight title at Fusion night club. That was one of those fights where experience told. No matter how hard I tried, I could not put Mark away but, over three rounds, I beat him to take the title. Mark Greener is an amazing bloke; one of those fighters who, at the bell, when hostilities end, I embraced as a brother-in-arms. I have nothing but respect for the man.

The thing is that, during this period, I can honestly say that I didn't care whether I lived or died. That is how messed up my head – my life – had become. I went into all those fights, and many others, ill-prepared and uncaring. At the bell I was putting myself in the hands of fate. Yes, I always had winning on my mind. I'm competitive by nature, right back to my football-playing days. The reality, though, was that I was abusing my body and deluding myself. By taking on good fighters in the physical and mental state that I had got myself into didn't do me, or them, any justice. I was denigrating the sport I love.

In saying that, I am not wishing to dilute their achievements, whether they beat me, ran me close or lost. They turned up full of intent, did their job and did it well. The real loser was our sport. When athletes pit themselves against their peers, the least they should expect is that the competition is playing fair and giving of their best. It is the only true and accurate measure of their accomplishments. I can't honestly say that during my coke-addicted years. All too often I was fighting when I shouldn't have been anywhere near a boxing ring. I lost fights I should have won. I won fights but don't know how. Most of what I did from the age of twenty until I got clean just over three years ago is a blur of drugs and the demons they unleashed.

It was disrespectful to our sport and to the men I fought and for that I apologise. As a result, three years ago I got clean. I vowed to myself that from then on my opponents would meet me at my best and the best man will win. To date, I have kept to that vow and, barring two draws, have kept a clean slate. Having acted so unprofessionally in the past, I still felt that I had a lot to prove. That was one of the reasons I decided to take off the gloves and have a go at bareknuckle boxing. What I hadn't reckoned on was that survival on the BKB circuit didn't only depend upon what went on between me and the guy I was fighting.

Joe Smith-Brown (aka Joe B-Bad), my first manager, you now know about. The next snake to sink his venomous fangs into me was the ill-named Christian Roberts: Christian by name, crafty by nature.

CHAPTER EIGHT

SHAMROCK, SHENANIGANS AND A SAWN-OFF

Loyalty and trust are two of the most important qualities in any close relationship. More than most athletes I would argue that a fighter really needs to believe in the people they work with. Fighting, be it gloved or BKB isn't just a physical contest, it is inherently dangerous.

When I look back now, I ask myself why, again and again I placed my trust so readily in people I barely knew. As if I wasn't doing a good enough job of fuckin' up my own head! I hooked up with egomaniacs who treated me with contempt. You'd think that after the Joe Smith-Brown experience I would have learned but no. I got through two more managers in rapid succession before I finally found someone I could rely on and who really believes in me and who is determined to help me realise my true potential. That person is Alan 'Macca' McDermott.

Loyalty and trust are not only key characteristics of Macca's character but at the very core of his principles. He doesn't give them readily. However, once you've earned his trust, you'll enjoy it for life. Macca will never let you down. Break faith with him though and you'll have lost a courageous and totally dependable friend forever. Ask a few of his former BCF sidekicks. Thirty years on, some are still like brothers to him, others, non-existent.

Under his guidance and management great opportunities have come my way. First and foremost, my dream since childhood, The Guv'nor title fight, as well as parts in two major films, an appearance in the Lenny McLean documentary and – this book. Yes, we were together when we met the writer and the relationship I have struck with him since has been fundamental *but* Macca was no less influential in cementing the bond the three of us share.

As with everything else, Macca studies the small print and handles the deals and details. I don't have to worry about what's going on behind the scenes, out of earshot or anything. All I have to do is focus on my diet, training and preparation – apart from the time spent working on this book. Then I had to jot down reams of notes and answer Stephen's endless questions, emails and texts. At times it almost got overwhelming. Not his constant pressing for information but; being forced to face my past in minute detail.

I'm a stress-head you see, and a worrier, but Macca takes everything in his stride. With his calm but firm, no-nonsense style; he seals the deals, diverts the dross and sorts out the inevitable shenanigans that are part and parcel of fight promotion. He takes the hassle out of my routine but keeps me, and my dad (out of respect and friendship) fully informed of all important developments. That's what a good manager does, that's what Macca does but as I said, not all managers are good.

How to characterise Christian Roberts? One word – snake! Just like Joe B-Bad before him this guy appears to have had a solitary, selfish mission that of creating a profile in the world of BKB. Once again, I was duped and used to achieve that goal. Christian managed my career for three short but eventful months. Just enough time to get his company CMS Promotions off the ground. 'Cheers, Decca. Got what I wanted. Now fuck off, there's a good lad!' He didn't actually say that, but he might as well have.

In the time we were together he arranged one fight – with Stevan Miller from Leicester. One of only two bareknuckle fights I ever contested that were declared draws, as previously mentioned. The build up to the fight and the unpleasantness surrounding it really illustrates what a sleazy and dangerous world BKB is and how, not matter how good a fighter you are, you have a lot more than your next opponent to worry about.

Christian Roberts was a publican from Warrington when we first met. That was in November 2014, at Joe B-Bad's Bradford BKB Show, which is an interesting craic in itself. I'll come back to that once I've got the Christian saga out of the way. Christian seemed a nice enough gadgey. We chit-chatted about this and that and, it became obvious that he was more than just a fan of BKB: he was looking to get his foot in the door.

Within a few days of the Bradford Show, Christian rang my dad to talk to him about becoming my manager. Had he picked up on the social media gossip about Joe releasing me?

Or had he tapped Joe at the show and got a heads up that I was about to be cast adrift? Again, these are questions I have never had answers to but those strange events, when taken as a whole, are riddled with coincidences.

What had become clear to me by then was that it was time to move on. Joe obviously had and he couldn't have made it any plainer. Once again I was a pro-fighter without a manager. After his chat with my dad, and a brief family pow-wow, Christian Roberts became my manager. He has always claimed that he slipped straight into his new role and hit the ground running by fixing up my next fight. He didn't. My name and my name alone secured that fight. Stevan Miller was keen as mustard to fight me, so the fight was on. All Christian had to do was have a craic with Jay Wann at Raging Bull Promotions then dot the 'i's and cross the 't's on the terms. A purse of three grand was agreed. Lovely – I got down to some serious training. It doesn't matter what shape you're in or how confident you feel, you cannot take a man like Stevan Miller for granted or he'll pound you to a bloody pulp.

It was set for 31 January 2015: me versus Stevan, all 6ft 8ins of him. A proper tasty fighter who tipped the scales at an impressive twenty-two stone. The pre-fight build up via social media very quickly became heated and offensive. Stevan was goading me and trying to get into my head by making crude comments about, and directly to, a girl called Taylor, who I was seeing at the time. His strategy worked too. He couldn't know but you do: I hate bullies and despise men who assault women. I was bound to react. OK, these were verbal assaults but targeting Taylor was well out of order. It really upset her and her family.

As a consequence I soon began to hate that man. This was

going to be war. One of those rare occasions when I would climb into the ring with the explicit intent of doing as much damage as possible to my opponent. Not my usual mindset but I felt I had to punish him for all the insults he had aimed at a girl I cared for.

To prepare for the fight with Stevan, and a subsequent fight with David Price, I turned to Pat Mulroy. Pat's a cockney who lives in Galashiels, in the Scottish Borders. I call him the Cockney Jock but don't you take that liberty should you ever meet. He's a cracking bloke and what you see is what you get. Not what I'd call 'a people person' though; grumpy with zero tolerance for time wasters and piss takers. Pat's a man who seems to have the hump with the whole world. Yet (when not in the jaws of that Black Dog, I'm a happy-go-lucky lump) we got on like a house on fire.

We'd meet at a gym in the nearby town of Hawick. A beautiful part of the world by the way, if you've never ventured into the Scottish Borders, it's time you did. There's a lot more to Scotland than Edinburgh, Glasgow and the Highlands. Carlisle to Hawick and back involves a round trip of ninety miles along winding roads and on a slow bus. Nice scenery though, which is a good job, because I made that tedious journey without fail or complaint three times a week, all on account of one thing: Pat's reputation. He is a genuine fighting man, boxer and a trainer who really knows his stuff.

In the period between November 2014 and when the fight was scheduled for, January 2015, Pat got me into tremendous shape: super-fit and razor sharp. Pat's permanent state of anger must have rubbed off during those gruelling sessions. His simmering rage and snarled instructions filled the space like really dark-mood music which, in turn, drew furious effort out of me on bag, pads and during sparring sessions. The routines he put me through would flash by in a frenzy leaving me completely knackered. Often as not, I was so whacked when I caught the return bus that I'd sleep almost all the way back as it rocked, bucked and bounced through that rugged border countryside.

It was all worth it though. I went down to Leicester in great shape and really up for taking on big Stevan. So a huge thank you to my coach. You're the business Pat. You were there for me when I needed you. If you're reading this mate, and you ever need Decca, call me. I'll be there for you.

Christian was spot on during the build-up to the Miller fight. He said all the right things and appeared to be very busy getting to know everyone on the circuit. He was expanding his network and, let's not forget, his own profile. All his big talk of getting me some serious sponsorship, however, proved to be bullshit. Just my luck; I'd hooked up with another gobshite who did nothing more than talk a good job.

During his three month stint as my manager it also became clear that he thought of himself as a bit of a gangster. In actual fact, he was a pussy. Trust me – I know the difference between the real thing and the plastic variety. BKB draws all kinds of scallywags, villains and gangsters into its orbit. The pretend ones stand out like a wig on a pig. The reason being that pretence requires having to act the part and the real ones don't need to act – they just are!

Another of his unsubstantiated claims was that he'd competed in twenty-eight amateur boxing matches. If so, I've never come across a single person or found any records to substantiate his claims. Not only that, in an interview after we'd parted company he claimed that he'd moved on to resume his own fighting career. Interesting. How many fights have you had since leaving Team Decca, Christian? What's that? None? Zero? Zilch? You need a good manager mate. Know any? Sadly I'm left to conclude that Christian's another dreamer, another wannabe whose sole achievement has been setting up CMS Promotions on the back of being my manager for a very short time. Do you detect a pattern forming?

Let me now draw this sorry episode to a close by telling you about the actual fight with Stevan Miller – the one that Christian took credit for arranging but actually happened because Stevan wanted to fight me and Jay Wann of Raging Bull Promotions made it happen. It did not take place thanks to Christian's consummate negotiation skills. In fact, his flapping and lack of bottle damn near cost me my fair share of the purse but I'm getting ahead of myself again.

Stevan was being represented by Jay Wann. Let me make it quite clear at this point in this story that, I do not hold Jay responsible for anything that happened. He's a decent bloke who always does his best for the people he represents. Jay did just that and Christian did his thing. The trouble was that Christian was clueless and hopelessly out of his depth, which was never better demonstrated than when, on the eve of the fight, we got word that the purse had been cut by a half. What do you suppose my 'gangster' manager did about that last-minute liberty? Fuck all!

We were there, I'd prepared and I wasn't going home empty handed no matter how weak Christian was being. The fight went ahead with Barrington Patterson refereeing.

Stevan had underestimated me. I suspect he'd watched my early fights against Bulldog which, I'd won but not with any great panache, and the two Americans I beat with relative ease. Between those fights and ours though, I'd put a lot of work in and was a very different fighter. The first round went the way most do, both of us feeling our way, testing each other's defence, but as the fight progressed, I could tell that Stevan was surprised that he couldn't put me away. I was taking his best shots and catching him with some belters too.

Fighting a man with a height, weight and reach advantage is always tricky and Stevan is no slouch. He knows his ring-craft, so I had to do a lot more backpedalling than I would normally do, not least because Stevan adopts a similar stance and style to me. He was relentless and kept pressing forward the whole time. On top of that, the man is massive, so going-toe-to-toe to try to match his attack would have been suicidal. All he would have had to do was stand tall and pour it on as I tried to get underneath those long powerful arms and huge fists. I had to be patient: bob and weave and pick him off with counter punches while keeping mobile. Stevan kept trying to cut me off and pin me in the corners so as to launch a barrage and he almost did a few times.

As the fight was drawing to a close I sensed he was tiring. I started to press but I left myself open and he caught me with a peach of a right cross. It stung but that steel jaw of mine withstood it. I shook it off, nodded my appreciation and touched knuckles with him in salute. That's about acknowledging your opponent's skill, showing respect, it's what gentleman fighters do.

At the final bell Barrington stood between us and raised both our arms – a draw. He's the ref and, that's the result, but if look at the fight on You Tube you'll see that I am barely marked. Stevan has a face like a butcher's block and a broken hand but I'm not complaining. It was a hard fight against a very big and hard man. He landed some great shots. What did rankle was that they tried to stiff me over the purse.

A three grand purse and drawn fight means £1,500 each. Jay wasn't for giving me more than £750. After all the bad blood during the build-up, I'd anticipated that there might be trouble afterwards, being as how Christian had cocked up the negotiations and I was in Stevan's backyard. What was I to do? I couldn't take them all on to get my money.

Fortunately for me then that I had, let's call them: Terry Allsorts, Rog Lion and Gary Jeeves along for support. What can I tell you about Terry, Rog and Gary? Not much that I can put into print. Suffice to say, they're 'faces'. The real deal – and not the sort of people you'd be advised to take liberties with. Anyway Rog, not my manager, you will note, worded Jay up with a little help from another geezer in the back of a black Range Rover who was holding a sawn-off shotgun.

That wasn't in the script, just Rog ad-libbing. Never mind Jay, *I* was absolutely bricking it when I saw that. Rog told him straight: 'The purse was agreed and Decca gets what he was promised.' In fact, Rog was so annoyed at them that he got cheeky and asked me if I wanted the whole three grand. I said no. I'm not a greedy man and I'm fair minded. The fight was drawn, half the purse was what I'd earned, was what I was due and all I wanted.

Jay coughed up but I hope there are no hard feelings. I had not asked those boys to negotiate on my behalf but you know what these guys from The Firm are like – they don't like to see a friend get rumped. Cheers, boys.

With my earnings in my arse pocket I headed home and I'd barely got through the door before Christian bailed on me. Had my 'gangster' manager bottled it when things got a little tasty? I'll leave you to draw your own conclusions. Whatever his reasons, just like Joe before him, he walked away from a winner. What is that about?

I believe that it was the very next day that he set himself up as CMS Promotions. So that was the second BKB promotions company kick-started by a no-mark, with no pedigree in BKB who had taken the Decca Heggie route. Once again I was on my own. Hardly any wonder I get a little paranoid but thankfully, by that time in my life, I'd turned my back on drugs and alcohol and embraced faith. Oh yeah. Full of surprises aren't I? Yes, it began after a chance meeting with a priest in the grounds of Carlisle Cathedral, at one of my lowest points.

It was only three weeks or so before my first bareknuckle bout with the Leicester Bulldog which came out of the blue after I'd mentioned to a lad called Tucker Thompson that I wouldn't mind a crack at that. I believe it was Tucker who passed my name to Andy Topliffe and the rest as they say is history.

If you'd seen me that day in Carlisle you'd have never believed that a few weeks later I'd be winning my first bareknuckle fight. I was lost within myself, in the grip of a torturous depression and wandering aimlessly around the city centre. Looking more like a tramp than a future champion, I passed through the grounds of the Cathedral.

A stranger's voice said, 'Can I speak to you, sir? '

When I looked around, there was a young priest sitting on the wall. He asked me my name and I told him, then he gestured for me to sit beside him. After a short chat he led me into the beauty and tranquillity of the cathedral. We talked about my issues for about twenty minutes before he said, 'Where do want to be in five years? '

In all honesty, I couldn't answer him but that question sparked something in me. Then he held out his hands and made upturned fists and said, 'In my left hand I hold the past. In the right – the future.' He made a throwing motion with his left hand and said, 'I'm chucking away your past.' Then he opened the right hand and showed me his empty palm. 'Now go and find your future, Derek.'

From that day I took responsibility and ditched those bad habits and addictions that had kept me down. I began to read the Bible and found an inner-peace I had never known before and it was all down to a chance meeting with that priest. Or was it really chance? My new found faith tells me different. Someone is always watching and listening. All you have to do is open your mind and heart to the possibility. That day faith and self-belief replaced cocaine and alcohol. Determination replaced despair. Once again I dared to believe that I would realise my dream. One day I would be The Guv'nor.

The brief meeting in Bradford, which eventually led to Christian taking over as my manager, happened a week before I was supposed to be flying to the States, for a third time. On that occasion I was supposed to be taking on Mixed Martial Arts (MMA) star and Ultimate Fighting Championship (UFC) Hall of Fame legend, Ken Shamrock in a bareknuckle contest. Once again Joe had pointed me Stateside to, according to him, further my career.

That week proved to be one of the strangest and more sinister times in my short BKB career. Not long after I agreed to fight Ken, my parents started to receive menacing phone calls and death threats from someone with an Irish accent. The caller said that they would blow up our home if I went to the States. Why was a Decca Heggie vs Ken Shamrock fight such a big deal that people were willing to make death threats to stop it going ahead? It didn't make any sense but to be honest, not a lot of what was going on around that time did.

Like I said, my head was wrecked. One minute I wanted to take on the world, the next I wanted to hide from it and everyone. I was yo-yoing from hyper to utter desperation. The 'closed door' managerial style Joe had adopted was fuelling my paranoia.

Based on what I've already told you about Dad, you might have guessed that he isn't easily intimidated. Had he got his hands on the cowardly Irish c**t on the other end of that phone, he'd have shoved his bomb right up his arse and pulled the pin but – he had his family to consider. What if the threat was real and his grandkids were visiting when the bombers struck? He couldn't take that chance and so, I asked Joe if there was anything he could do.

Joe B-Bad had made a lot of useful – but what you might call, dodgy connections, through B-Bad Promotions and the murkier sub-culture surrounding BKB, but even he seemed a bit mystified by the whole thing. He told me not to worry and that he would make a few calls. That's what I wanted to hear. When he got back to me he claimed that he hadn't been able to get to the bottom of it and had no idea who or what lay behind the threats. All he had was what I already knew: Ken Shamrock is of Irish-American stock. *Durhh!* The guy calls himself Shamrock?

Joe figured that maybe former IRA heavies or another Republican Dissident faction had got in on the game. Perhaps the betting wasn't filling the right pockets or the odds weren't keen enough. Had a betting syndicate skewed things and made Ken's people nervous? We were left to speculate but the bottom line was that we couldn't be sure, one way or the other whether it was a serious threat or just a cruel hoax. Joe advised me to pull out of the Shamrock fight. 'Why take the chance?' he reasoned. Why indeed? I agreed. It was no big deal, he added reassuringly. Another fight would be arranged soon enough.

Joe said everything I needed to hear at the time. Obviously, he was looking after my best interests as well as those of my family, so a phone call was made and the fight was off. I, in turn, let my dad know that I wouldn't be going to the States and that should keep the people making the threats off our backs. Sorted. Sure enough, no more threatening phone calls were made to the Heggie household.

Unbeknown to me though, within ten minutes of my conversation with Joe, in which *he* had advised *me* not to fly to the States, he had posted a notice on social media that I had 'bottled' the fight with Ken Shamrock. His statement went on to announce that: 'Decca Heggie will no longer be associated with B-Bad Promotions.' You could have shot me in the bollocks with a police Taser and I'd have felt less of a shock. Talk about a stitch-up. Saville Row wish they had Joe on the needle and thread.

So much for his reassurances and the promise to fix me up with another fight; utter bullshit. Clearly he had no such intention. Once I'd recovered from the shock and disappointment I was absolutely bouncing. My manager had gone from saviour to career assassin in the space of ten minutes and – surprise, surprise – he wasn't returning my calls. The snide bastard had used the situation to ditch me. To this day I have no idea why.

In a further twist, it turned out that Ken Shamrock wasn't

completely sold on the idea of fighting me either. In an interview posted on You Tube, he cited my inexperience as reason for his reluctance to agree terms. I've often wondered since: did Joe B-Bad already know that Ken's team were backing out before he advised me to withdraw? Had he been looking for an excuse to pull me from the fight all along? Was the idea of paying my expenses to travel to the USA bugging him? Was the purse inadequate or not in place? Did he upset the Yanks and had the negotiations turned sour? I don't know because I've never had answers to those questions and I doubt I ever will. Speaking for myself, had it not been for the death threats, I would have been ready to board that plane and fight Shamrock on his home turf.

The great Ken Shamrock however, wasn't willing to 'get it on' with a relative novice, having fought and won at the highest level in the octagonal ring. At least that's what he says in that interview. An odd decision if you ask me, given that he has no track record to speak of in BKB. Make no mistake, his MMA and UFC stats speak for themselves but bareknuckle boxing is a totally different game. I accepted his decision but not his reasoning. If anything, with my EBF background and three victories already chalked up in BKB; two of which were in Philadelphia, I felt we would be pretty evenly matched in a stand-up straightener. Not only that – I'm fairly sure I would have taken him.

CHAPTER NINE

TWICE
THE PRICE

The hardest BKB fight I've ever had was my first encounter with Big Dave Price at Rotherham in June 2015. This was a coming together of James Quinn McDonagh's Knuckle Promotions and Andy Topliffe's Pit Fight Club. The name James Quinn McDonagh is synonymous with bare-knuckle fighting. Everyone in the game knows him or has heard of him, if not as a leading promoter then as a fighting man in his own right.

We're talking about a fella who was once known as 'King of the Travellers': a title earned by pitting himself against the best from the gypsy and traveller tradition of the sport. Are you getting the picture? James has seen it, done it and ripped the fuckin' T-shirt off at more tear-ups than most and against some of the most renowned bare-knuckle warriors. He might be knocking on a bit nowadays but beware: he's still got a fist like a cannonball and enough spark in his fuse to fire that missile to great effect. You have been warned.

My opponent that day, Dave Price, is a really cracking lad with a massive heart but he's a complete savage inside the bales or a boxing ring and, at Rotherham, he hurt me. Yeah, I know, that's bareknuckle boxing, it always hurts, but Dave took the usual pains of combat to another level. I have never taken punishment like it before, or since. Worse still, when we faced each other, it was under a cloudless sky on one of the hottest days of the year, in thirty-five degrees. In that heat, over five torturous rounds, our endurance was tested to the limit. We both suffered that day. As if that wasn't bad enough, guess who was appointed to referee the bout? Stevan Miller, who I'd fought to a draw not long before. That's BKB for you: full of surprises.

I travelled down to the show with my cousin Neil Parkin and my dad. What I hadn't told them was that, five weeks before, Gareth 'Gumpy' Walker, one of Pat Mulroy's people, had cracked one of my ribs with a killer hook while we were sparring in preparation for the Rotherham Show. So unbeknown to them, I hadn't been able to do any core work, sparring or much else in that time.

Not being one for making excuses, despite a cracked rib being a legitimate reason to pullout, I went there full of intent. Never once have I gone into a fight expecting to lose and I knew what would be said if I had cried off. The BKB network is absolutely rife with snipers and shit-stirrers. Somebody would have immediately started accusing me of bottling out. Ever since my dad geed me to take Jamie on, I have never bottled or dodged a fight with anyone, be it on the street, in the bales or in a boxing ring. I'd rather lose honourably than be branded a coward.

Once I started making my living as a fighter, my attitude

became more focused and professional. If the money isn't right, I will decline a fight until they up the ante and, if they don't, they can pay some other mug the pittance on offer. Once I've agreed, I'm there, whether I'm primed or out of condition.

Back to Rotherham and the very dangerous Dave Price. I can remember clearly our Neil saying, 'You don't look a hundred per cent, cuz,' as we walked through the crowd towards the bales, and he was right. I was ill-prepared and out of condition.

In the opposite corner, though, Dave was looking tuned up to perfection and very menacing as he paced and shadow-boxed. Check him out on YouTube. The man's built like one of those Greek statues and is as hard as the marble they carve them from. As I said, a real nice feller but, Jesus Christ Almighty, you do not want to get into a staring contest with him. He looks proper evil when he's in the zone and he was wired for action, every solid inch of him a mean and hungry, bareknuckle savage beast. Fuck it! We hadn't driven all the way from Carlisle for nothing. Worst case scenario: I'd be hurting for a few days afterwards. A few days? Try weeks!

At the off, he charged into me and caught me on the left temple with a lump-hammer of a hook. It felt as if my head was coming off when it landed and rattled right through me to my toes. Within seconds, up popped a lump like a goose egg. One shot I'll never forget. For a good few seconds I had the wobbles but those good old Heggie genes saw me hold fast. Nice one, Dave, mate. I still cringe when I watch replays of the fight.

That furious start from big Dave got the crowd going and soon the Carlisle contingent were in good voice.

'Mahh-sheeeen, Mahh-sheeeen. C'mon, Decca.'

123

I always appreciate the support, folks; truly, it means an awful lot. Yet, as I've said before, I hear it but have other stuff on my mind. Sorry, no time to stop and give you all a wave. Dave was in ferocious form. He dominated the next round as well but, in that square, under that blazing sun, it quickly became clear to me that I had the better engine. I let him rattle away at me so as to burn up his reserves, offering sharp counter-punches in reply. Dave had gambled on a quick finish but we battled on and on. Sure enough, he began to tire. Fatigue is a bitch when you're fighting. Everything goes to rat-shit: timing, power, reflexes, balance.

By the end of the third round, I felt that I'd gained the upper hand. I also knew that I had more fuel left in my tanks than him but I'd broken my right thumb. In the same way that he rocked me in the first round, I began to punish him with a few beauties of my own and every right-hander sent a searing pain up my arm. As the fight wore on, Dave took three twenty-second standing counts(in bareknuckle fighting, the count is twenty seconds, not ten as in gloved boxing).

Then I caught him with my best shot – a crunching straight right to the mouth. A show-stopper, thank fuck, 'cause it hurt me as much as it hurt him. He backed right off as far as the bales allowed, spitting blood all over the place, but Dave Price is a fighter to his core. He carried on gamely and aggressively until Stevan, thankfully, called a halt. Five gruelling rounds in heat that would have left a camel gasping and the referee's decision? Cue fanfare – a draw! *A fuckin' what?* No, I'd heard him right.

All sorts flashed through my mind. Granted, I had a bump above my temple that made me look like I was growing another head, a broken thumb nobody knew about but me, and a few scuffs and bruises. Oh yeah, and I'd poured so much sweat that the spectators were wading through it but Dave had a mouth like busted tomato, even more bruises *and* had taken three – *count them* – three twenty-second standing counts.

Seriously, Stevan? Okay, whatever you say, ref. Sportingly, I accepted his decision without complaint and Dave had given almost as good as he got. Bitching about it is pointless, ungentlemanly and demeaning but I confess that it left a bad taste. Don't forget that my bout with Stevan had also been declared a draw and, on that occasion, I also felt that I had edged it on injury tally alone. Throw in the three standing counts and, to my mind, there is no question. I won.

To add insult to injury, Andy Topliffe tried to rump me on the purse and held £250 back. Well, my dad wasn't having that. He gave the fucker a tug and told him to cough up. These might be bareknuckle promoters and fighters themselves but, trust me, when my dad looks at you in a certain way, you pay attention. Sensibly, Andy handed over the rest of my winnings and we were on our way.

We hadn't been on the road long when I got a call from Stevan on my mobile and he apologised. He admitted that he'd called that result wrong. It's funny how, in hindsight, he was able to reach that conclusion because I don't think there were many at that fight that thought he'd got it right. Stevan Miller has never fought Dave Price and I know who I would put my money on if it ever happens. I've wondered since if Stevan just didn't want to declare me the winner against a man he has never faced and doesn't fancy his chances against. Only a theory, not an accusation – and there's one way to prove my theory wrong, Stevan: fight Dave Price. Twice, like I have.

That's another frustrating feature of the BKB scene. There are promoters, managers and even fighters who go through all kinds of antics to avoid meeting certain fighters and others who seem to do all their fighting on Facebook. They craft a rep based on bullshit, aspersions and sly innuendo. People such as Andy 'No Fear' Shithouse – *sorry*, Hillhouse – of Glasgow, for example. For three years that gobshite has accused me of dodging him.

It began thanks to Christian Roberts of CMS Promotions' incompetence. He was supposed to have been arranging a fight with this Glaswegian wannabe but was unable to secure a licence to hold an event at his base in Warrington. As a result, Andy was all over social media claiming I was avoiding him. You might be reading this thinking, 'Sticks and stones, Decca, lad. Why let it bother you?' I'll tell you why. You are nothing without credibility in the fight game. You can only ignore an idiot like that for so long before it really does seem to be the case that you're dodging a fight.

It became such a pain in the arse that my dad contacted Andy's manager and made them an offer. We'd have a bareknuckle straightener, on the Q-T, on his home turf, in Glasgow. Each of us puts in five grand and the winner walks away with the full purse, ten large. No fuss, no expensive venue or ticket sales, just two fighters, our managers, our corner men and hard cash from our own arse pockets. Do you suppose Andy was tempted? No! Apparently, he was too busy with his acting career. You got that right, Mr Hillhouse. All that bollocks you posted on the Internet was nothing more than an act.

As far as I am aware, to date, his bareknuckle career consists of one fight against a Patsy who has never won a bareknuckle fight. Hillhouse? Glasshouse more like – the minute my dad tossed a rock their way with a note tied to it, his bluff was shattered.

In the time that elapsed between my two fights with big Dave Price, I'd got through three managers but so far I've only told you about two: Joe Smith-Brown and Christian Roberts. Macca had been following my career, just as a family friend and boxing enthusiast, for quite some time and was always there with a little sage advice whenever my dad or I turned to him. Then one day he invited me out for dinner and we had a great craic about what had gone before, and about my ambitions. As ever, he was genuinely concerned and full of sound advice.

Unlike the others I'd dealt with until then, he understood my motivation. Not only that, he truly believed in my ability. Now Macca's one of the most direct people I have ever known, apart from dad maybe. He can be very blunt but he's never rude. He's honest and tells it like it is without fear of hurting anyone's feelings. It's another reason why he gets on so well with my dad: two peas in a pod. They don't suffer fools. They don't have egos and won't massage anyone else's. If it happens that you don't handle the cold, hard truth very well, don't ask either of them for their opinion.

For the life of me, I cannot think why but it had never occurred to me to ask him to be my manager. Perhaps it was because he was right under our noses: a mate, a familiar face. Maybe it was because we knew he had other business interests and was not one for spending time away from his family. I wish to hell we had thought of Macca earlier. It might have saved me a lot of hassle and disappointment. As it was, someone else also had managing my career in mind. *She* had been easing her way into my confidence via social media for a while: Nina 'The Black Widow' Cranstoun.

I'll devote the bulk of the next chapter to the very striking but sly Black Widow – that's her own nickname, by the way – but the reason I have flagged her up now is because she was on the horizon at the same time that Macca's growing influence came into play. In fact, her part in my story overlaps with Macca's and Christian's to some extent. During her brief spell with Team Decca, I had, in effect, two managers. The official one being Nina and also the ever reliable, but unofficial, Alan 'Macca' McDermott. Christian was still about, pestering us, as he tried to grow his new promotions company, CMS.

As you might have gathered, my head's all over the place, partly on account of self-inflicted damage. My mental state was being regularly tested, by the way, so many others have conspired to stall or destroy my career. There have been times when I have felt like I am not just taking on the fighters but the whole BKB movement. And here was naïve little me thinking I'd entered into an honourable brotherhood with blood ties. An admirable warrior code.

Haydock near Ashton-in-Makerfield was the venue of my rematch with Dave Price. This was more than just a rematch, mind; it was billed as a UK Heavyweight BKB title bout. Three things got me to that event: the opportunity to settle the score over the Rotherham draw that never was, the title belt that was on offer and the promise of a decent purse. What almost put me off was that it was another CMS Promotions event. True to form, Christian didn't have everything squared away. Never mind the old cliché 'couldn't organise a piss-up in a brewery' – and he's a former pub landlord – based on my experiences at every event he's promoted, he couldn't organise a fun-run for circus clowns. Worse still, he'd be the biggest joker there if he did. It probably won't surprise you to learn that CMS Promotions has since gone into liquidation.

During the build-up to the fight, Christian was going around beating his chest and the jungles drums, in part to boost ticket sales but also to take every opportunity to diss me by telling everyone that I couldn't 'live with Dave Price.' You've got to wonder if he'd even bothered to watch the first fight on YouTube but that's Christian for you. He lives in cloud cuckoo land. If he had the slightest grasp on what this game's about, his company might not have folded.

I'll hold my hands up. That sort of shit does get under my skin but what my enemies and rivals don't understand is this: taking the piss, taking liberties, ignoring my record, disrespecting me as a man and a fighter only lights my fire. Come the fight, they're facing someone who not only has the tools to take them down but a point to prove as well. Good job getting me revved up, boys. Thank you. I should really have a 'Do Not Press' warning sign and a big red button on my forehead. Maybe then they'd get the message? In a bareknuckle bout I don't lose because I don't know how to lose – it's just not in my psyche. I am wired to win and my detractors merely give me a greater incentive.

Our first fight had been a brutal slugging match in which we'd both suffered, not least from heat exhaustion. For this one, Dave was clearly taking no chances. He'd trained and sparred with the very classy, former professional cruiserweight Carl 'The Cat' Thompson, holder of WBO, IBO, British and European titles, and it showed. This man chalked up two wins over Chris Eubank, beat David Haye and recorded only six losses in his professional career.

If this had been a McDonagh or Topliffe or even a B-Bad Promotion, we'd have been met by a big raucous crowd but it wasn't. It was a poorly attended CMS event. Dave received an even more lukewarm reception than I had as he entered the club. My supporters had, at least, given me a decent gee and were still making themselves heard. Despite the MC's best efforts, he failed to stir the punters up. There was real tension. After the inconclusive first fight, we had something to prove and there was more at stake.

Dave, who is impressive at the best of times, looked confident, sharp and hungry as he entered the ring. We were called together and given the usual talking-to by the ref. A respectful knuckles-touch and mutual 'tattie' tap of the fists and we were ready to rock. Just as he did in Rotherham, at the bell he tore into me like a maniac in the first round and had me on the back foot. He was combining haymakers with sharp hooks and jabs. I had to rely on my steel jaw and counter-punching to survive the first couple of minutes. Towards the end of the round, he was blowing a little but I had energy to burn. The longer a fight lasts, the greater the odds are that I'll win because I can stay on my feet and still be swinging after ten rounds, twelve, whatever it takes.

In round two, though I decided to step it up and take the fight to him. This time I dominated from the bell. I stung Dave with a couple of crisp jabs and hooks but this is one very tough man. When countering, Dave wasn't proving as effective as he when he launches his all out attacks and I caught him with a cracking right to the chin that put him down. I'd opened up a nasty gash in his chin that needed six stitches after the

Above: I always thought football was my calling in my school days. Look carefully to spot my dad next to me – a true hard man (back row, third and fourth from right).

Below: Hiking in the Lake District. Given our dodgy trainers, getting up that mountain was a proper test!

The curtains aren't the only thing to have changed over the years. . . Not bad biceps for a six year old, though!

Train like an animal, fight like an animal: getting in some heavy chest work before my brutal fight with Stevan Miller (*below*).

Showdown between the bales with Clifford Gray: I respect every man brave enough to stand his ground opposite me and fight. It takes some proper stones and, in my eyes, they are all warriors – win or lose.

© Darren Greysho

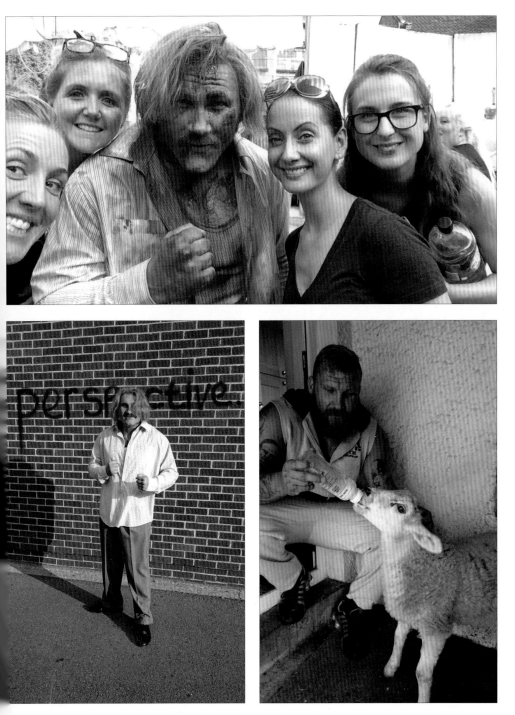

Above: Me as Blockie Johnson, scaring the girls behind the scenes of *My Name is Lenny*. Josh Helman did an amazing job playing the great Lenny McLean, and I was able to give him a few tips on real street-fighting in our scene! © *Stephen Wood*

Below left: No matter which way you spin it, life is all a matter of perspective. © *Stephen Wood*

Below right: It's not all bloody knuckles though: Buddy the lamb is a real champ – my good friend Stephen Wood and his wife nursed him from the brink of death… and then the unlucky bastard had to hang out with me! © *Stephen Wood*

Above: My amazing team, suited and booted, ahead of the biggest night of my life. I wouldn't be where I am today without these people.

Below: Two men who were firm friends in the days running up to the Guv'nor fight: on the right, Macca and I (outside the Hippodrome club in London, where Lenny famously used to work the doors) and on the left, my co-author Stephen Wood.

Above left: From one hardman to another: it was a genuine pleasure meeting Paddy Doherty on the train down to London for the Guv'nor title fight. What a legend.

Above right: This is my moment. I stand, a proud man, with the Guv'nor belt around my waist and the mic in my hand, telling it like it is.
© *Stephen Wood*

Below: The Guv'nor Belt: a lifetime to earn it – seconds in which to win or lose it.

© *Stephen Wood*

Henry Rollins once said 'there is no better way to fight weakness than with strength' – in my life, the black dog of depression has had me down, but never out. If we can find the strength to stand tall in our hardest battles, life can never get the better of us.

© Darren Greysh

fight. Dave took the count on his knees but got up, chest now painted crimson, claret dripping from his chin. He came at me again.

In bareknuckle fighting, you have to park your conscience until the fight is over. I was fighting a brave man; someone I admire. He was bleeding heavily but wasn't ready to lie down and so my job wasn't done. Sorry, Dave, but you'd have done the same in my shoes. I slammed a few more into his ripped face, which sat him on the ropes. The ref sent me to a neutral corner while Dave took another count. I was watching him like a hawk, willing him to stay down. I didn't want to do him anymore damage but I would if he stood. He didn't, thank Christ. The title and belt was mine. Being the true fighting man he is, Dave Price came straight over to my corner to congratulate me and give me a hug. You're a gentleman and true warrior, Dave, and a real hard, scary bastard to face in a fight.

All of a sudden, Christian Roberts was all over me. Dave was history; I was his man again. I told him to fuck off and pay up. Big surprise: he only had £400 of my £1,500 purse. Ticket sales had been poor, blah, blah, blah. . . You don't say. An optimist would argue that it was a case of 'standing room only' but that was because there was no fuckin' seating. Those who were standing, well, let's just say they could have safely held a cat-swinging contest. It also went some way towards explaining why some of the punters looked like rent-a-crowd. He'd probably had to discount and give tickets away to swell the numbers. If it hadn't dawned on Christian by then, though many others in the know had realised, he wasn't really cut out to run a promotions company.

Having worded the arsehole up, I took the 400 notes and then spent another four weeks getting the balance out of the useless twat. Unfortunately, that wasn't to be the end of my dealings with Christian 'Wannabe' Roberts. If we thought the second Dave Price fight was a pantomime, which on no account had anything to do with Dave, 'The Battle of the Bales' was a total fiasco. However, I'll save the story of the fight for later. As you might imagine, with Christian running the show, we got messed around from pillar to post before I finally stepped into the pit to face Clifford Gray – and when I did, it was a cesspit!

By this point, I was drug, alcohol and steroid free. With Macca guiding me, I was beginning to realise my potential. The road to redemption stretched way ahead into the distance but that bastard black dog is always snapping at my heels.

CHAPTER TEN

BLACK DOGS AND BLACK WIDOWS

I've been putting off talking about this but I did say I would tell all, so let's recap. Throughout my twenties, my head was in absolute shit order. Bordering on suicidal half the time, off my scope the rest. Even my mum's devotion and endless patience eventually reached breaking point. Losing Becky had sent me off the rails; getting arrested and convicted for 'inappropriate touching' turned me into a complete train wreck. I wasn't handling that conviction at all well.

Guilty – end of, that's all people read, see and hear. They weren't in court to hear my side of the story, not that the magistrates had any sympathy. I'm not making excuses but I think, had they dragged a few folk in off the street to listen to the case, they might have thought, 'There but for the grace of God go I.' Instead, the Chairman of the Bench made his decision and a simple, playful arse slap became a conviction for indecent assault and the stigma that carries.

I walked out of that court feeling pretty hard done by and proper dirty. It felt as if everyone was pointing and whispering about me behind cupped palms. 'Keep away from that dirty bastard. He can't keep his grubby mitts off women's arses.' At least that's what I was hearing in my head every time I made eye-contact with anyone. That feeling persists. Lesson learned. I swear to God, your backsides are perfectly safe when within hands' reach, ladies. And, gents – yours always have been.

Yes, I held my hands up but I didn't realise the seriousness of what I was admitting. That's the absolute truth. It probably didn't help that I was coked off my tits when I stepped into the dock. I was still in a state of shock that it had ended up in court and, as stupid as it sounds, cocaine was my crutch. Some folk would have a quick fag to calm the nerves; I'd chop a couple of lines of Charlie. Despite the fact that – or perhaps because – I was buzzing, when questioned by the prosecution, I told the truth.

My happy-go-lucky self died in that dock. As if my three years ban from working the doors wasn't bad enough. Surely there was no way back from being branded as some kind of sex-pest by that bloody newspaper? The Black Dog had me well and truly cornered. I turned in on myself and to the only comfort I felt I could depend on: coke and alcohol – big style. I know. Talk about making a bad situation worse. Even after I'd served the ban and resumed working security, my addictions had such a hold on me that it got worse. More money in my pocket meant more Charlie and more Scotch.

Mum finally lost it with me when she found a wrap of coke in my bedroom. Visions of the drugs squad booting our door in and ransacking the house were the last straw. So that was it: I was out, but not on my ear. Mum couldn't bear the idea of me dossing or sofa-surfing. So, with dad's help, she made sure I had a proper place to crash. For £50 a week, I rented a friend's gaff over in New Harraby. Although it saved them the stress and tension of sharing their home with a coke-headed depressive, it meant that I was free to do as I pleased. I did.

For a while there my routine comprised of: wake-up, walk to the bakers and buy something to eat for my breakfast, go back to the house, snort four or five lines of Charlie, start a bottle of Scotch, maybe take a shot of Deca-Durabolin, or Sustanon and testosterone, do a bit more Charlie and Scotch, maybe some Valium or Tramadol, pass out – and, when I eventually woke from that stupor, start all over again.

If all of that wasn't bonkers enough, I was growing increasingly unpredictable, brimming, as I was, with steroids. Days drifted into one another. I was wasting my life but the Charlie and booze kept telling me I was having a great time, for a while anyway. Then reality began to bite and depression got me in a headlock. All the same, as messy as I was, I never actually went looking for trouble. Or is that just what I told myself? Probably, because during those lost years, trouble always seemed to be around the next corner.

Perhaps the 'on-off' switch temper I'd developed didn't help, especially when I was potless and running low on drugs and whisky. Then it only took the lightest of touches to take me from sad-man to mad-man.

What a good job then that most of the company I mixed in back then were not the type to go running to the police. In our world, there are only two things worse than a grass and they are paedos and beasts. What I'm saying is that I could kick off at the slightest provocation and give some deserving, or less deserving fucker a good digging without seeing the inside of a police cell.

Occasionally, my victim, having licked their wounds, might have a crack back at me with a sly bottle or glass. If they did, they got a proper hiding. Working on the doors, I've seen the some horrible injuries caused by nasty bastards using beer glasses and bottles. So when someone comes at me with one, there will be no quick thump and goodnight; I do a proper job and wreck them.

The other sort who couldn't let it lie would maybe round up a few mates, or send just one pal who fancied himself as a little bit tasty to even the score. That never worked. Whoever it was would rarely end up thanking his friend after they'd caught up with me.

'OK! Who's comin' to A&E with me, boys?' That was my attitude. One, five, ten? I didn't care. I'd take the lot on.

I've never forgotten the bloke who dropped me and stamped on my head when I was fifteen because I'd knocked out those three lads. So I get proper pissed off when some would-be tough guy comes looking for me to settle the score for someone else. Listen to me. To the wimp who sent him: if you're not man enough to fight your own fights, don't fuckin' start them. To the idiot they sent to sort me out: choose your friends more carefully!

To be honest, though, there weren't that many repercussions. I might have been wasted and coke-head 99 percent of the time but, by then, I'd developed quite a fearsome rep. Most lads took a clump from me without too much complaint. In the main, they weren't all that different from me, you see, brought up on rough council estates where casual violence was a way of life. I had lived with the fear of it but learned to accept it before I was ten years old. Most of the other lads I knew had the same mind-set. You win some, you lose some. I just didn't lose many.

My situation, though, was aggravated by the fact that I really didn't give a fuck about the threat or outcome. That fatalistic attitude made me very dangerous to be around. Promising, fun-loving youth to paranoid, angry man-child in five, or was it six, easy steps? Been there, done that, stole the T-shirt to sell for drugs.

You do what you have to when you're an addict. A bit of 'bobbin', weavin' and thievin' – yeah, I'm afraid so. These are the sorts of things addicts resort to feed that need. I was more of an opportunist than a professional tealeaf. I never broke into people's homes or anything like that. Leave something lying around that I could lift and sell for a bit of Charlie, though, and it was gone. The proceeds of petty crime shoved up my nose or poured down my throat. Pathetic, isn't it. Looking back, I'm ashamed to even think that I'd stooped to that level.

Then there was the debt-collecting, which I've already covered. Working the doors proved another source. It brought unsuspecting coke dealers and users into my orbit. Frisk, slap, seize and send them on their way. Snort the Charlie they had planned to sell and then wait for the next mug to come along. I'd turned into the kind of monster I'd absolutely hated before that drug took over my every waking moment.

Drink and drug addiction turned me into someone I didn't recognise or want to know. A nasty stranger I couldn't stand the sight of and definitely didn't want to share my head with. So much so that I decided to get rid of him. There was a beam spanning the ceiling of the livingroom in the house I was renting. It looked sturdy enough to take my weight. So I knotted a tie around my neck, stood on a chair, threaded it over the beam, secured it and kicked the chair away. I dropped and just about brought the whole fuckin' ceiling down with me. The beam snapped and I crashed onto the floor in a pile of debris, a pathetic, blubbering wreck, and the room wasn't much better. My landlord was not a happy man when he saw the mess I'd made.

Suicide attempts are often dismissed as attention seeking or a cry for help. That's not what I was doing. Help? I didn't want help. I wanted out. And I'd made sure that there was no one around to suddenly rush in and stop me. I didn't call anyone or leave a note for someone to find either. I meant it. Had that beam held, I'd be dead. Now you might think it corny but I took the fact that it didn't as a sign. Once I'd stopped blubbing and I'd dusted myself off, I went straight around to Mum and begged her to take me back. After swearing on my life that I'd stop taking cocaine and cut out the drinking, she agreed. Little did she know how genuine that oath was.

Mum took me at my word and I moved back into the family home but Dad took a lot more convincing. Poor old Dad. He knows I can work my mum but, to keep the peace, he gave his consent and even squared up his mate for the damage. Of course, I didn't tell them how I'd brought that beam and part of the ceiling down. I think I told them I'd been trying to do chin-ups.

It felt great to be back home and I immediately began to sort myself out – but there was still the occasional relapse.

Depression is something I have lived with since my early twenties, maybe earlier. I'd probably dismissed it before then as teenage angst – you know, bad moods, everyone getting on my nerves. Blame takes on many forms when the Black Dog is on your back and depressives are the worst self-analysts ever. They can't see through the mental fog. My upbringing played no part in my slow-burning, meltdown but I perhaps can apportion some to Jamie and his crew. The main reason for my depression, though, is most definitely drug abuse. A combination of recreational drugs and steroids fucked my head up. Now that I recognise and accept that, I want everyone to know: don't blow out your brains searching for a buzz. I know that campaign fell on deaf ears where I was concerned but 'Say no to drugs' is the only way. You know it makes sense.

How do I describe its affect? Like I said, I'm not exactly hot on self-analysis but I'll give it a try.

Have you watched the Harry Potter films? If not, you must be the only bugger on the planet. Anyhow, they're good films, so fuck off sniggering at big tough Decca watching the boy wizard while I get on with the craic.

There are these hideous, spooky, flying creeps called Dementors that turn up in the third film, *The Prisoner of Azkaban*. These things attack their victims by holding them in a hypnotic grip that's impossible to break free from (unless you're Harry Potter, of course). Then, using a mouth that's like an unwiped arse with teeth, they suck out the souls, the life force, energy and essence of their victims. At least, that's what I make of what is going on when they strike. When their done with their victims, there's nothing left – just a zonked out, empty shell of the person.

That's what depression feels like to me.

I have sometimes wondered if J. K. Rowling was ever a

depressive. I don't mean she seems like it, but wouldn't be surprised. You'd have to have been there and done that to come up with an idea as accurate as those Dementors, eh? Anyway, no more Harry Potter craic from here on, so you can stop pretending you've never watched them.

Knowing that drugs caused my problem is the reason I'm very reluctant to take drugs to bring it under control. To date, I've only used Valium to bring me down off coke but not to help me cope with depression and I've never consulted a doctor or asked for help. My situation is self-inflicted. Why should anyone else, through the NHS, foot the bill? Anyway, that Black Dog doesn't scare me. Oh yeah, he still corners me from time to time and takes a sneaky bite out of me but I deal with it better these days and emerge stronger after every dip. Anyway, dogs don't live as long as humans, so the smart money is on me. The day I feel that I cannot fight my way out of that corner, I'll go and see my doctor.

Don't think you have to do it my way, though, or face it alone. There is help out there. Start by telling someone you trust or go to see your GP. If you don't want to go down that route, there are some great support networks for depressives like us, such as SANE or that Heads Together project Princes William and Harry kicked off not long ago. Give one of them a call and talk to an advisor. Talking about it is only the first step but it's the biggest one you'll have to take. After that, it gets easier.

You might find that people begin to respond to you better after talking to them. By revealing your true self, they may understand that you're not a weirdo or some unpredictable headcase, but just a regular person who is trying to deal with a mental health problem. Speaking of which, I must have needed my head examined when I agreed to let Nina 'The Black Widow' Cranstoun act as my manager.

The Black Widow: where do I begin? Nina is all woman – alluring and shapely, with an all-over tan, a sleeve of tattoos and the sultry good looks of a Mediterranean siren. Better seen than heard, in my opinion, but, unfortunately, she likes the sound of her own voice. She must do: she talks a lot but says very little. It pours out in a crackling southern accent that raked this northerner's eardrums like the point of a nail on glass.

Well-named the Black Widow because she is deadly and I, like others before me, wandered blindly into her web. She runs a promotions company called Touch Gloves that was once the property of a cracking bloke called Ricky English, who now runs EBF. Ricky has a solid reputation in the fight game and was one of the promoters of my Guv'nor Title Fight at the Clapham Grand in October 2016.

The other was Joey Pyle Jnr, son of the underworld legend Joey Pyle, and, like his father, Joey Jnr is a promoter and a true 'mover and shaker' on the circuit. His father before him handled my hero Lenny McLean *and* Lenny's arch-rival, Roy 'Pretty Boy' Shaw. Some say Joey Jnr isn't like his dad. Yeah, well, who is? I'm certainly not and times have changed but, believe me, Joey Jnr has enough of his old man about him to garner respect and, when he turns up anywhere with the sinister but trusty Freddie G at his side, people sit up and take notice.

I felt privileged that the son of the man who oversaw Lenny's blood-curdling climb to the top of the unlicensed fight game promoted the fight that saw me lift that coveted Guv'nor belt.

Nina wheedled her way into Touch Gloves in much the same way as Joe Smith-Brown did with B-Bad Promotions. Do you sense a familiar pattern emerging? Different methods, same result: a foot in the door quickly followed by a foot up the arse. Loyalty isn't in the dictionary for these people; it seems to be a luxury they cannot afford.

Ricky is a total, twenty-carat diamond. Like Macca and Mr Feeney, my old Maths teacher, Rick's another one of those Ronseal geezers: 'He does exactly what it says on the tin.' Where the fuck did Mr Feeney just pop-up from? It just goes to show that, when you're a positive influence in someone's life, you are never forgotten. In years to come, I hope that someone mentions my name out of the blue like that; that I will have made a similarly favourable impression on other people' lives.

Back to Ricky: an experienced, no-nonsense promoter and former Olympic boxing coach who lives and breathes the fight game. Somehow though, the Black Widow got her dainty feet under his table and, before you know it, she was the new owner of Touch Gloves. And Ricky? Having been bitten, he took the antidote and went on to bigger and better things. I may hold the title but I have him to thank for staying true to the fighters' and promoters' code, unlike so many others. What a tremendous job he did staging that Guv'nor event. I have nothing but respect for the man.

So as I said, Nina lured me into her web via the World Wide Web. Social media is a great communication tool but it's a specialised bit of kit that, in the wrong hands, can just as easily break as many things as it fixes. We'd been exchanging messages for a while, which eventually led to her asking for my phone number. Screen time immediately became cosy chats and it didn't take long for her to get to the point. She wanted to represent me and predicted great things if I agreed. It soon became clear that Nina could not only have sweet-talked a Trappist monk out of his cell but out of his robes and onto the hen-party circuit as a Strip-O-Gram. Well, I'm no monk but I must have been a mug. In my defence, I was fairly desperate.

There I was treading the shark-infested waters of BKB, having been cast over the side by Christian Roberts, when two lifebelts landed within easy reach. Macca was one but he hadn't actually mentioned being my manager at that point. Nina Cranstoun, who had thrown me the other, was talking management so, naturally, I grabbed at hers and before long had signed up with Touch Gloves.

You have to understand that I'm a fighter, not a businessman. I lack the experience and confidence to manage my own career. Nor did I have the patience, skills or desire to deal with the complex negotiations promoters get into when trying to arrange an event. Not only that, I was still pretty new to the game and I did want to fight. I wanted to be a champ and, ultimately, The Guv'nor.

The reality was that, as with Joe and Christian before, Nina saw me as her way to exploit the potentially lucrative BKB market and position herself where she loves to be – front and centre. I'd done it again: signed with a manager who was more interested in their own profile than that of their fighter.

Ironically, one of Nina's favourite words was 'longevity'. Funny then that she only hung around for four months, which, as it happens, is the life span of a dragonfly. Imagine that: a life lived in four months, birth to death. Well, that was the life span of my career in her hands: longevity my arse. She was always dropping things into conversations about her strategy for my career. All of which never amounted to much more than waffle and empty promises.

In that time, she arranged one fight. She had equalled Christian's woeful record but had taken a month longer to get there. Four months: that's her definition of longevity in action. Unfortunately, arranging a fight is one thing; staging it is another, and, just to put the icing on the cake, in the opposite corner, representing my opponent, was the man himself, Christian Roberts. It was to be held at the NE6 in Newcastle: a rematch but this time a gloved bout between me and my most dangerous adversary to date, big Dave Price.

The fight was publicised widely, with posters printed, and the tickets were selling reasonably well. Speaking of publicity, it didn't escape my notice – nor that of many others, I'm sure – that Nina's image was always prominent and larger than that of any fighter she was promoting. It certainly hadn't escaped Macca's attention either and, without trying to undermine her, as a friend and advisor, he did question her priorities more than once. More and more I was heeding Macca's advice and, although he was being diplomatic, I could tell that he was not impressed. However, I gave Nina the benefit of the doubt, believing that she deserved the chance to prove herself. And prove herself she did. Black Widow? Black Mamba more like.

With four weeks to go to the fight, she posted a status on Facebook to the effect of 'Due to Decca Heggie's behaviour, I am having to pull out of this event.' I was stunned. What behaviour? All I had been doing was training in preparation for the fight. All of a sudden, I was receiving angry messages asking me where all the money had gone? I was baffled. What money?

After a couple of calls, I discovered that all the money from ticket sales had disappeared. I'm not accusing Nina but I absolutely and categorically deny that it had anything to do with me. In fact, never at any point did I have anything to do with ticket sales or the taking of money for tickets. I get tapped up all the time for freebies but never have I sold tickets to one of my fights. That's the promoter's job. Touch Gloves was promoting the event, not Decca Heggie. As for me, I never saw nor touched a single penny of the ticket money that was paid by the punters.

Meanwhile, my manager was not returning my calls. Instead, she began posting messages on social media suggesting that I'd had it away with the cash. Not once did she level that accusation at me to my face, or even in a phone call. I wonder why. I'll leave you to draw your own conclusions. That situation had repercussions I was still reeling from weeks afterwards. Of course, Christian Roberts latched on to her accusations and was driving much of the sniping. He even played his 'I'm a bit of a gangster' card in an attempt to intimidate me. He arranged a face-to-face meet to thrash out this missing money business. I had already explained at length but I wasn't going to have him put it about that I'd refused.

Christian wouldn't be satisfied until I produced my personal bank statements and then only reluctantly. Then the cheeky twat played his ace. He had recruited Stephen 'The Devil' French from Liverpool to ride shotgun. Stephen's a well-known debt collector and 'face' around Merseyside. He's not a man to mess around with so, when they turned up, ignoring Christian, I strode right over to him, held out my hand and said, 'Hello, I'm Decca.'

Stephen shook my hand and Christian may as well have sucked his thumb because that was that. I told him once again – and for the last time – that I did not nick the ticket money. Stephen believed me and Christian was left with no choice and mumbled some pathetic stuff about having it out man-to-man. Really, Christian? So how come you brought the infamous Stephen 'The Devil' French along? Man-to-man obviously doesn't mean one-to-one in your book, eh? Since that meeting, Stephen French and I have formed something of a friendship. He's a nice man to know but maybe not such a nice man to cross. Knowing Stephen as I now do, I'd say that I'd much rather have him as a friend than an enemy.

All that suggestion and suspicion from the same man who, when *he* rescheduled and promoted the Dave Price rematch in December 2015 at Haydock, was shy by £1,100 on the purse and then took a further four weeks to produce the money!

Of course, Nina was never to be seen again in my circles. I, for one, will be delighted if it remains that way for a very, very long time. Reflecting on my time with Nina, I'm left to conclude that her definition of longevity is based on the life cycle of an ancient and beautiful insect. Maybe she should change her nickname from Black Widow to Nina 'The Dragon Fly' Cranstoun. As for the missing money, your guess is as good as mine. I offer only this fact: I didn't do-a-runner, or turn off my phone, or resort to snide social-media innuendo. I stayed put, faced my accusers and proved my innocence.

This sorry tale of incompetence, betrayal and theft ends on a happy footnote. With Nina on her toes and out of the picture, and with my dad's blessing, Alan 'Macca' McDermott stepped up to take control. From that moment, I've grown as a fighter and, finally, have begun to realise my true potential.

It hasn't all been plain sailing, though. Macca's a canny bloke but he's had his work cut out handling me on account of the moods and the insecurities I live with. Not least because I've been had over so many times. What really stands out under Macca's management is this: unlike the other three, he's not one for the limelight. He puts my interests first. Not only that, he's always thinking ahead and prepared for the unexpected. A fact that was never better demonstrated than when Christian Roberts tried to line up a fight between me and Clifford Grey, another respected veteran of the bareknuckle circuit.

CHAPTER ELEVEN

BATTLE OF THE BALES

Nina was history and Macca was my new manager but Christian Roberts and his CMS Promotions company were still lurking in the background. Christian was keen to set up a fight with Clifford Grey and, as it turned out, with good reason. CMS was a basket case. He sweetened the pot by making it a title bout: The CMS Bare Knuckle Heavyweight Championship. Naturally, with Christian running the show, my fight with Clifford Grey had all the usual elements of a farce. I suppose, considering the havoc in Haydock last time around, courtesy of Mr Roberts, we should have known better but I fancied my chances against Clifford and what can I say? I'm a sucker for a title and belt.

I feel that at this point I should add that Macca *did* know better. Reluctantly, though, he gave in, if only to shut me up, but he then took every conceivable precaution once the deal was agreed. Even then, Macca had to be at his wiliest best to match Christian's twists, turns and dodges. Setting it up involved God knows how many phone calls and texts between him and Christian. Good job Macca's a cool customer – Mr Unflappable. He was not about to let Christian have his way.

It all began during a trip to Bradford Bulls Rugby League Club as guests of Rob Parker. Rob's a professional rugby-league prop-forward with an impressive club portfolio and international honours to his name and, as it turned out, something of a fan of mine. Dad, Macca, Dave, my pad-man and trainer, my cousin, Anthony Heggie(or Smeggie, as he's known) and I all set off for Bradford. We had been on the road less than an hour when Christian phoned Macca, who rolled his eyes and put the phone on loudspeaker:

'Hi, Alan, it's Christian. I want Decca to fight Clifford Grey for the Pit Fighting title. The purse is a grand.'

Macca said, 'Thanks for the offer, Christian, but Decca is the champion and has beaten your best man [David Price]. His name sells out your event and venue and I think he's worth more. Stick another five hundred in the pot and we've got something to talk about.'

Macca also explained to Christian that he hadn't taken our expenses, such as travelling down to Haydock, into consideration. What Macca had said was all true. Christian knew it but negotiation never was Christian's strong suit. All he got in response was, 'It's not my fault you live in Carlisle.'

You've got to wonder if this wannabe really thinks Warrington is at the centre of the universe. It's not even the centre of England. Macca politely declined the offer on the grounds that I was worth more – and he was right. Christian had never shown me any respect and was, once again, with his derogatory offer, taking the piss. Everyone agreed that Macca was right to decline.

Christian's parting words were just plain weird. 'To quote a famous Prime Minister, Alan, "The Lady is not for turning."' What sort of bloke tries to impress fighting men with Thatcher quotes? Churchill, if you must quote a politician, but Maggie? Whatever! As usual, Christian was talking shite and the bitch did turn – no, he rolled over and grudgingly coughed up the extra £500. Of course, all that happened a few days later but his derisory earlier offer didn't spoil our day out with the Bulls.

At Bradford, we were all greeted like VIPs and I was treated like a prince. The staff and the players at Odsal Stadium really made us feel very welcome. I came away with the feeling that we'd made some really brilliant friends at a great rugby-league club with a fantastic rugby tradition. It turned into a truly memorable day, not least because I also met Robbie Hunter Paul, a total legend in the rugby-league world and a proper gent. He was the David Beckham of that code, the Ronaldo of rugby league, and he took the time to make me feel not only welcome but like one of them.

I sometimes wonder if I would have become a good enough rugby-league player to reach that level and grace places like Odsal had I switched codes that day when Macca first approached my dad about me training with his junior squad. I certainly had the size, heart and engine. That's why I became a champion fighter. Rugby league is, at times, like a thirteen-aside bareknuckle brawl. And like true hard-men, after the game, winners and losers pat each other on the back and shake hands.

On the road back to Carlisle, still buzzing after a truly

memorable day, Macca's phone rang again. It was James Quinn McDonagh offering me a spot on his Newcastle show. This time the hook was a showdown with Cowboys McDonagh – so tough his nickname's pluralised. That's my take on it but, to be honest, I don't really know why he calls himself Cowboys, rather than Cowboy. Unlike Christian, when James Quinn McDonagh makes an offer, it's always genuine and worth serious consideration but Macca had a strategy worked out for me and told James he'd think it over. He didn't see how that show would advance my career. He was already thinking beyond BKB; beyond fighting as it turned out. Macca's a bugger for holding his cards close to his chest.

That was another novelty for me. I had a manager with an actual thought-out plan; a career strategy, in place. This sort of thing never happened under my previous management. Every one of the other three would have put me in the ring to fight King Kong for his peanuts. I wouldn't mind so much but I'm more of a pistachio kind of guy.

The chance to claim another title plus that extra £500 had me convinced. The cash top-up and title carrot saw me mither Macca a bit – OK, a lot – to accept Christian's offer. I still felt the need to prove myself and it had been a while. Macca's reluctance was partly down to his having to deal with the untrustworthy Christian and the fact that I had barely recovered from an illness that saw my weight drop to seventeen stone and five pounds. I would be facing Clifford Grey a stone lighter than when I enjoyed my sensational second-round win over David Price.

OK, so I wasn't truly match fit but I felt strong enough and was itching to put another CMS-backed fighter away. So Macca relented and, against his better judgement, made the call.

Come the day, the team gathered at Upton Langbrook, near Pontefract. A small but tasty crew consisting of me, Macca (no slouch in a tear-up) and my cousin Johnny Heggie: cool and calm with a hint of menace. Then there was Steve Anderson from Northampton, who fills his XL T-shirt nicely and would be working my corner, and Darren Diesel Grayshon, who, at the time, was the team photographer. Not forgetting Macca's old mate, Doddy from Carlisle: a proper useful lump of muscle to have around if things got lairy.

We decided to check out the venue first. Macca puts great store by the old saying 'Failing to prepare is preparing to fail.' He also wanted to scope out the area for a quick getaway if things did get iffy. They sometimes do at bareknuckle events. I'm telling you, it's not only the guy in the opposite corner you have to watch out for. All sorts of hard-cases and wannabes turn up. Quite a few, if not most of them, juiced and fuelled with coke and booze by the time the bell goes. Some of them are practically climbing the ropes or clambering over the bales to join in as the blood, temperature and testosterone levels peak.

When we got there, it turned out to be a run-down social club that resembled a pig-pen, already filling up with spectators. Don't get me wrong: I like a crowd; it gives the fighters a right gee up and lends atmosphere, but the general mood was that of rabid hyenas waiting to pounce on the one that falls. Another good reason to make sure it wasn't me that went down.

Underwhelming would be the best description of our collective reaction. This was back-to-basics, real grassroots stuff; the dingier end of bareknuckle fighting. Like a scene from *Shameless*. Now I'm an Old Harraby lad, rough around the edges to say the least; council-estate born and raised, as were Macca and the others. What I'm trying to say is this: we are all quite comfortable in the company of folk from the lower end of society – usually. The bulk of the punters milling about that spot, though, looked like they were in a holding pattern for the *Jeremy Kyle Show*! Or rejects turned away by the floor manager for being too scummy even for that exploitative c**t.

We were greeted with the odd welcome smile but mostly with suspicion and hostility and Macca decided I was better away, out of there until the fight. He proposed a quick peek at the marquee and 'the pit' and that we retire to the nearest pub or hotel. I can't remember which of the lads said it but we all chuckled when we heard, 'Fuck me, have we landed in that *Star Wars* bar?' muttered quietly from within our ranks. They needn't have worried. The force was strong with me!

Let's start with Christian's idea of a marquee and buffet, which consisted of a gazebo, which was probably stolen from Aldi or Lidl, and an Iceland buffet box. Oh, all right then: the contents of half a dozen buffet boxes you wouldn't feed a stray dog with. It was pitiful, as was 'the pit', if you could call it that. Let's face it, when a fighting arena, by definition, is called a pit, you don't expect the Coliseum but Christian's definitely didn't pass muster. It was an arse-wipe from being a septic tank: a few bales around the back of the building, formed into an eight-by-eight feet square. Worse still, the ground was a quagmire. Macca was disgusted and said, 'He's havin' a fuckin' laugh, Decca. You'd struggle to squeeze three fat kids into that space.'

Macca was all for calling the whole thing off. I think the

others thought he was right but I just smiled at him and said, 'I love it.'

They were all stunned but it's true. It felt right. Macca often asks me what planet I live on. Despite being as close as we are, we are also very different animals. Macca's steeped in the whole history and ethos of boxing and its noble traditions. He doesn't like the bareknuckle game at all, to be honest, and he's been trying to steer me away from it since he got involved. As for me, yes, I too admire – no, worship – the likes of Mohammed Ali but bareknuckle fighting isn't the same. It is raw and primal and it's not pretty and, if I wasn't so damned handsome, I'd have just defined myself.

Somehow, the rats' nest of a venue and the muddy pit seemed wholly appropriate; the perfect place for two men to meet in unarmed combat and fight until only one is left standing. The only difference from this and holding it in a boxing ring would be that, when Clifford went down, he'd be wallowing like a wild boar instead of lying on the canvas.

Clifford's a big and experienced unit but, despite not being in fighting prime, I wasn't too worried. For a big lad, I have real hand speed and enough power to make every punch count. The way I saw it, if I could put big Davey away in two rounds, I could surely cope with anything Clifford brought to the party. However, Macca soon identified a major problem. I'd brought boxing boots and, on that surface, it would be like fighting on ice. I'd get no purchase whatsoever. Where would the leverage for my big knockout shots come from? [They begin at ground level. I drive from the foot, up the leg and quads into the lats and shoulder, then fire the right arm forward into a thunderous jab.] Just staying on my feet would have proved hard enough, let alone counter-

155

punching while dodging Clifford Grey's snappy hooks and jaw-breakers.

Good old feckless Christian. The venue was a dive without changing facilities or privacy. The bales had been laid on slippery, soft ground. Only *he* would consider a dump like that, a suitable place to hold his big CMS Title Fight. Well, we were there and it was going down but how to make sure I didn't while wearing the equivalent of racing slicks on my feet? Macca suggested we make a sharp exit to the nearest hotel and discuss tactics. He got no argument. We needed a plan for the fight and a plan of action about getting out of there after it was over.

We found a half-decent pub and settled down when Macca had a brainwave. Football boots! Studs would give me the grip I needed but it was well after the time that any sports shop would be open. Even then, we had no idea where the nearest one was. Great idea but how to execute it? We scanned the pub. Light-bulb moment number two!

'Let's ask the punters,' Macca said. 'One of 'em might have a pair of size tens he's willing to flog to us.'

No harm in asking. We did a quick survey of the pub and Macca happened to ask a top bloke called Dave Smith, who was standing at the bar. Having explained our problem, Dave said, 'Leave it with me,' then drained his beer and was out of the door.

Dave is a veteran of a hundred-plus Muay Thai kickboxing bouts and, as it turned out, a Facebook friend of mine who had been following my career for a while. What were the odds? He told Macca that he'd recognised me when we walked in but he isn't the kind of guy to make out like he's your best mate just because our paths had crossed on social media. Dave turned out to be my best mate in Haydock that day, for sure, and has kept in touch since. In no time at all, he landed back with a pair of size 10 Nike Ronaldo 90 soccer boots. Perfect! We were back in business and all buzzing again. Dave had saved the day. In fact, I still have the boots in my room. What a cracking lad. If you're ever heading Carlisle way, mate, give me a shout.

We had about ninety minutes left to kill before Clifford was to find out the hard way what he'd signed up for. Macca took Steve, Doddy and Darren with him to that pig-sty Christian laughingly called 'the venue' to see how things were going, As it turned out, not too well.

We knew Christian of old by now. Macca wasn't having any of the nonsense we got at the Dave Price fight, where the promised purse turned into instalment payments. Fights were ending fast, more than likely because nobody could stay on their feet and, according to Macca, Christian had been acting all edgy. Anyway, Macca spelled it out for him.

'No pay, no play.' He wanted to see the money upfront or we were on the road again.

Christian huffed and puffed and promised, 'You'll get your money but I'm busy right now.'

Macca left him with a flea in his ear. 'You know the score,' he said and left Steve and Darren behind to keep an eye on the slippery bastard.

Macca landed back at the pub as I got ready with a little pad work, shadow-boxing and footwork. Dave and Macca were trying their level best to get me riled up to dish out some serious hurt but I never do, I never have. I know my job and I know that, once we've tapped fists, I'll get it done. Inside, my stomach churns and my ghosts return: Jamie and his weasel mates teasing me, flicking burning dog ends at me while they've got me cornered, calling me fatty, tripping me and slapping me around the head. Fear wells and, by the time I face my opponent, rage will have replaced it. The cold, clinical machine in me will unleash its fury.

The time was fast approaching and Doddy phoned. 'Hey, Macca! Better make sure you get paid, mate. This twat looks as if he's ready to fuck off.' Those alarm bells only Macca had heard began to ring loud and clear. We got our gear together sharpish and were about to shoot down there when his phone rang again. It was Christian.

'Hello, Alan.'

'What's the craic, Christian?'

'Err, well, I've got to go to the hospital. I'm pissing blood. Alison's got Decca's money.'

Macca just looked at his phone and then at us two. Christian had hung up.

'There's a rabbit off, Decca. I'd sooner trust Tony fuckin' Blair with a white flag in his hand than that c**t.'

We both knew what that meant. Talk politics with Macca and his opinion of our former prime minister will become clear; low enough to be found anywhere between the U-bend and sewer. Macca parked a good hundred and fifty yards short of the venue so we couldn't get blocked in if we had to be on our toes. He hurried ahead of us to find out what was going on and if Alison really did have the money as promised. It wasn't looking good. Christian had fucked off. Nobody could find Clifford Grey. When Macca did find Alison, she was surrounded by about five other agitated blokes.

Christian had bailed and left her in charge of this event

(if you could call it that) and, according to him, she held my 'coin'.

'What's the craic, Mack?' I called out when I caught up with our Johnny in tow. He didn't answer but elbowed his way through the mugs who were haranguing her. She assured him that she had the money and took off, promising to be back five minutes later. I was already stripped and ready to go to war but there was no money to be seen and no Clifford. I was about as pissed off as a scalded dog – and I was getting cold. Macca and Johnny had a confab. They were of one mind. No pay, no play. Not only that, Macca had promised my dad that he'd never see me ripped off. When Alan McDermott makes a promise, you can take it all the way to the Pearly Gates and St Peter himself will say, 'Macca said so? Fair enough, son.'

We were about to call it a day when two handy-looking blokes appeared. I'd seen them around before. Clearly, these lads had taken as many shots as they had dished out in their days. I saw Johnny and Macca exchange looks but I recognised one of them: Terry Allsorts. Yeah, one of the three geezers who had helped to get my purse money for me after the Stevan Miller fight.

Tailored in a sharp suit and sporting a gold chain you could exchange for a two-up, two-down in some parts of Carlisle, Terry looked well out of place among the scruffy, knuckle-dragging cavemen that had greeted our arrival.

'Awww'ight, lads,' he chirruped, with a distinctly southern twang. There were handshakes all around but they hugged me like I was family and then got straight to the point. They'd rumbled that we were going to walk but they'd come to see me fight and they were determined they would.

'What's it gonna take to get Decca into those bales, Macca?' Terry asked.

Macca wasn't sure but I told him that these guys were 'faces'; respected faces who could be trusted.

'Let me have a word with Decca's dad,' he said. Whether Macca was impressed or not is hard to tell. He is not easily impressed and nobody can intimidate him.

'You're wasting yer time, Pal. I'm acting on his instructions.' Macca replied. He wasn't bullshitting.

Terry called my dad and handed Macca the phone. Dad trusts this man but, if the money isn't there, the fight's off.

Then Terry's mate (who was wearing more gold than Tutankhamen) dug in his pocket and produced a wedge. 'A bag of sand. That's a grand to you,' he said with a smile that somehow didn't exactly radiate warmth. Terry got all excited and rubbed his big hands together. Macca remained cool, calm and impassive.

It turned out the bloke with the bankroll in his keks was Adam Croft, a jeweller by trade and very well known in his field and respected further afield, if you know what I mean. Adam might well have been a jeweller but he looked every inch a twenty-four carat handful, like a big, bad American Bulldog that chewed the whole fuckin' wasps' nest and spat the little bastards out 'cause their stings were tickling his tongue.

'C'mon, boys. Let's get Decca into that pit,' Terry said with a chortle.

Macca nodded his appreciation and said, 'Sorry, lads. That's not what we agreed.' He looked to me and Johnny. We nodded our agreement. Then a third bloke strode over who had been lurking just a short distance away, ear-wigging. This fella told us he happened to be Christian's cousin, then he pulled out another bunch of notes and started peeling twenties off. He handed them to Macca, who counted them and with a curt nod. The fight was back on.

We marched down to the pit *en masse* to chants of 'Old Harraby, Old Harraby.' It was lovely to hear. A bunch of my young followers from the estate had arrived. As they do, they were making their presence felt and their voices heard. It had started to rain but I couldn't have cared less. It was time and, after the delays and frustration, I was proper geed up for a scrap. The spectators were gathering eagerly, swelled by Carlisle pride.

Clifford followed me over the bales and squared off. He's not what you'd call athletically built but this feller has gypsy blood coursing through his veins and a bareknuckle pedigree that spoke for itself. The ref was Karl Harrison, no slouch in the pit himself, sporting a Mike Tyson-style tattoo on his face.

The only word that springs to mind as I recall that day is 'primitive'. The cruddy venue, the dodgy-looking punters, the shit-hole of a pit, big, rough Clifford Grey; even the ref looked like a fuckin' cannibal. All the same, after the chaos Christian had left behind, everyone was eager to get this thing started. Karl brought us together and gave us the familiar talk. We tapped knuckles, I stepped back, threw a couple of air shots to stretch my arms and shoulders, and Clifford raised his fists. Game on.

I steamed into him with a quick one-two and he went down. I immediately reached out and took his hand to pull him up. 'C'mon, Clifford, man,' I said quietly. 'Keep fighting.'

He shook himself and caught me with a big right in the side of the head. I walked right through it and put him on the bales again with a vicious combination. This time, he shook his head. He didn't want to continue. It was over. All that tension and fannying about for what? The easiest £1,200 I've ever earned, as it happened.

As the crowd dispersed, I saw Macca talking to a big lad who had posed for a picture with me earlier. Apparently, the fella said he loved me but wanted to fight me. Macca had that look on his face he gets when confronted by these types; either pissed or missing a few tiles from the old rooftop. I shook my head and wandered away with the others, surrounded by the Old Harraby Massive. The poor fuckers had travelled all that way to see their hero fight for a couple of moments. I looked back. Macca gently brushed the dust-monkey off and followed.

Back to our sacred border city, booty in my pocket and football boots on my feet. Battle of the Bales? Bareknuckle bedlam more like, all courtesy of Christian Roberts, but, for me, just another day at the office.

CHAPTER TWELVE

WHAT PRICE FAME?

Achieving my dream of winning The Guv'nor title and lifting that belt, attending fund-raisers and charity nights as a guest speaker, working on a book about my life, appearing in a documentary about Lenny McLean and acting in films: would I be doing this without having gone through all the shit that came before? The years I fell prey to callous bullies, the stupid stuff – the glue-sniffing and drug taking, the drunken, coke-fuelled, street-fighting years, doing jail-time – and then the black-tie-nights and bareknuckle fights, and so many other misdemeanours and mistakes? No! None of the things that followed would have happened. These things forged the man I have become and hammered me into shape on the anvil of life.

That said, neither would any of these things have happened without Alan McDermott stepping up to take control of my career. I was on the verge of quitting the whole fight scene until Macca got things back on track and restored my self-belief. I had begun to doubt myself but he never wavered. Having someone I respected as much as I do him at my side, telling me I had what it takes: that's made all the difference.

All the same, if I could turn the clock back and never have taken this road, would I? In the blink of a fuckin' eye! I swear to God. Along the way, I have hurt too many people I care about, let too many good people down and lost the love of a very special person. What has happened since will never fully compensate for any of that. I have accepted responsibility for my behaviour and mistakes. I have tried very hard over the past three years to put some of the wrongs right, not least in living a better, cleaner, healthier life.

Very few people live their life according to a grand plan or manage to stick to their plan if they do. Apart from those who are fortunate enough, by accident of birth, to be led from the cradle via prep-school, public school and university directly towards the Yellow Brick Road and a life of luxury. And some of them, with all life's advantages, still manage to cock up.

The reality is that none of us know what might come along that might knock us off the path we have planned to walk. Granted, I never really had a plan, unless you count the brief spell in which I thought I'd become the next Eric Cantona. Derby County opened their door and what did I do? I bottled it. So that was not so much a plan as a pipedream. At fifteen, I didn't have the courage or confidence to see it through. By the age of seventeen, a career-ending injury burst that bubble for good.

I thought I had a future as an everyday Joe and a life partner when I met Becky but I managed to blow that as well. It seems to me that I had to fuck up in order to buck up! Even then, I have come very close to blowing it all through ill-judged actions and comments that, in this instant-messaging, social-media age, can spiral out of control at the click of a mouse.

It doesn't bother me that people say I'm not the best; not the true BKB champion or Guv'nor. The stats and the facts bear me out but they're entitled to their opinion. I do take issue, however, with those who say these things while ducking and diving; who go out of their way to avoid taking me on. If you're a fighter and you think you're better than me, stepup and prove it – I did. I never have and never will offer any excuses. I took on David Price while out of condition and ill-prepared. Because of a cracked rib that had not quite healed, I was prevented from doing any serious training for five weeks leading up to the fight. Then I broke my thumb in the third round but fought on through the pain. Those are the extremes I will go to, rather than duck out of a challenge.

Non-fighters reading this will probably think that I'm punchy or some sort of masochist. Fighting men – the real ones – will recognise my attitude, though: we don't cry off or quit until we fall. Even then, most of us get up again and again before we finally acknowledge that we're beaten. I can say that because I go into every fight quite willing to die in a bid to win, as do many others, no doubt. As it is, though, I've never been beaten in a bareknuckle bout and that 'fight to the death' mind-set hasn't been put to the ultimate test and, hopefully, it never will.

The other thing I have no control over is the conclusions people jump to and what is said about me by gossips and trolls.

'He's The Guv'nor and held two heavyweight, bareknuckle titles. Therefore, he must be a mindless thug.'

Not true. These days, I'd go out of my way to avoid a fight, other than meeting my professional obligations. In my free time, I read a lot – poetry mostly – and I write the occasional verse too. I love the countryside and wildlife. I'm fascinated by anything to do with astronomy and the mysteries of deep space. As a former player, I am still football crazy and hate to miss my Saturdays in front of the box, especially the half-time and full-time round-up reports. Socially, I don't go out much but, when I do, I'd much rather be greeted by a handshake than a head-butt. Nowadays, fighting is just my job, not something I do for fun. Getting hit by some of the guys I've fought is no fun: none of us are in it for the laughs. In hindsight, I deeply regret the years when I did go up town intent on a tear-up.

My past behaviour is part of the reason that, in some quarters around Carlisle, I'm regarded as a bit of an animal. People have long memories but I'm not the same man I was then. You see a hint of the old Decca in a boxing ring or pit but, after the bout, I'm as easy-going a fella as you could possibly meet.

Sadly, some jealous types would have you believe very differently. Only recently I had a friend phone me to say he'd had to defend my name in a café. Some smack-head had marched in claiming I'd been jailed for kidnapping an ex-girlfriend and abusing her. Where did he get that load of bollocks from? My guess is the Internet and, of course, there are those who believe everything they hear or read without access to a single shred of evidence. There's isn't any truth in it, by the way. In fact, when my friend phoned me with that story, it was a new one on me. That was the very first time I'd heard that particular piece of fabrication but I doubt it will be the last, now it's out there.

While working on the book, I received a phone call from a trusted source naming the man who paid £2,000 to another guy to troll about me being a paedophile. The name of the one who coughed up two grand to destroy my reputation did not surprise me but, judging by the support I receive, very few people swallowed that lie either.

That is a prime example of the sort of shite people write about me. Utter rubbish that is completely without foundation or even the faintest element of truth. The trouble I have is this: among some of the fans of unlicensed and BKB fighting, I enjoy a minor-celebrity status. That engenders jealousy and, as a result, there are those who try to do me down and even deny my status as a champion. I sometimes wonder if that is where these carefully spun half-truths and, more often, complete lies are generated. I know for a fact that I would have had to have been in two places at once to have done some of the things I have been accused of doing.

I don't ask for accolades or attention but I do attract both. For example, quite recently a pretty young girl approached me outside a café. I was enjoying a latte with a couple of mates; one of them was her uncle. He introduced us and made a bit a big deal about me to her and so she asked if he would take a picture of the two us together. She handed her smartphone to him and, in front of my other friends and passers-by, I obliged. Arm around her shoulder, smile for the camera as her uncle took the photograph – job done. We shook hands and I asked her to share it with me on Facebook.

Within a couple of days of that happy snap, I was being publically accused of having done time for kidnap and false imprisonment by some heroin-addled idiot relative of the lass *and* of grooming her. And why? I am told that she had announced to her family that she was in love with me and was going to live with me! I kid you not. She had no idea who I was until her uncle told her. Such are the pitfalls of having even a minor-celebrity status in this age of instant fame.

Let's face it: these days, people become overnight 'celebrities' after failing to get on *X-Factor*, for Christ's sake. Not for winning but for appearing on the auditions and making a complete arse of themselves. Next thing, they're splashed all over magazines and billboards, opening new stores, posing for selfies and pimping their 'fifteen-minute fame' for all it's worth.

Thank goodness my good friends were there to defend my name and actions that day. One very brief meeting and by agreeing to take part in a photo-op and I'm branded a predatory monster. For a start, she came over to us and she asked for the picture to be taken. Not only that. She was nineteen and a single mum! Her uncle told me that himself and so she was not a juvenile and no shrinking innocent girl – the whole truth and nothing but the truth! We had our picture taken together. No headline, no scandal, folks! Can we please move along?

Is it any wonder much bigger celebrities are forever in the civil courts suing newspapers and Internet gossip-mongers? Attain any sort of public profile and it seems everyone is immediately out to get you. So if you hear any horror stories about me, do me a favour and stop me in the street and ask me if it's true. I promise that I'll answer you honestly, providing you're polite in your approach. Come at me like that fuckwit did, my friends, and I'll launch you into next week – unless you're a woman. Unlike some of the history's most celebrated professional boxers, so-called 'legends' of the sport, I don't hit women, ever.

I'd begun to recognise that my stock was rising when I was invited to speak from the ring at 'Train Like A Pro', an event held in the MK Dons Stadium at Milton Keynes and organised by Paul Saw. It was there that I first met Matt Legg, the heavyweight professional boxer who was in my corner at The Guv'nor fight and became a firm and trusted friend shortly after that first meeting.

The purpose of the event was to offer non-boxers eight weeks, under intense professional guidance, to prepare for their first boxing match. 'What a cracking idea,' I thought. Having never had any professional coaching, I nearly signed up for the programme myself. Joking! We'd been invited down by a former Guv'nor, 'Stormin' Norman Buckland, a house-end of an old pro and proud former holder of the title. Macca and I also found ourselves in the company of Eamonn O'Keefe, the film producer, and we got along like a house on fire.

Soon enough I was called up to speak and I must have been up there for about forty minutes talking about my life and fights. When I returned to the table, Eamonn told me how impressed he was by my honesty and ability to hold the attention of the crowd. The next thing I knew was that he was offering me a part in a film he was working on about bareknuckle fighters, set in the eighteenth century and called *The Bruising Field*. He dropped a couple of names, such as Tom Hardy and Mike Tyson, as potential stars and said he saw me in one of the leading roles as well. Macca and I exchanged knowing looks but humoured him by expressing interest but, to be honest, dismissed him as yet another bullshitter.

We get this all the time. The 'I've done this, I've done that' brigade who, truth be told, have actually done fuck all but talk a good job. For the record, Eamonn O'Keefe is not one of those people. Three days later he phoned Macca to tell him that he had popped the screenplay in the post. Macca hung up and rang me and said, 'Decca! This is real. That Eamonn fella is sending the script.' He did and it was a much bigger part but, hey, why not become an actor? Getting paid better for pretending to fight and feigning injuries than I ever was for actually fighting and getting really badly hurt? It's a no-brainer.

That is how weird my life has become. One moment I'm risking life and limb, smashing some mad, bad bastard around inside a ring of bales and the next I'm fending off outrageous and totally fictional allegations and then being asked to appear in movies with people like Josh Helman and the late Sir John Hurt. Will it get better or worse after I've appeared in these films? Only time will tell.

How did a troubled kid from Old Harraby end up in this situation? The short answer is: by never letting go of my dream. Even if you occasionally lose sight of it, never give up on realising your potential. I was a fat, bullied and terribly insecure boy with a gift for football, who had an outlandish dream: that one day I would be The Guv'nor. OK, genetics also played their part but, once I realised I had what it takes, I have pursued my goal ruthlessly. As is the nature of dreams, once you achieve them, other opportunities appear.

Since winning The Guv'nor title, I've focused on the two statutory defences and forging a career in film and TV. Such was the build-up to the on-off nature of The Guv'nor title fight, I've been playing it more cannily since. Dark forces were at play, rumours abounded, venues arranged and cancelled, dates changed and changed again. Ricky and Joey were messed about and wasted wads of cash getting tickets printed, only to see the deal melt away because some toe-rag had whispered in the ear of the Metropolitan Police about potential trouble, or got to the venue's owners. It was all very stressful for everyone concerned and I'm not sure I want to go through all of that again just to prove winning the title wasn't a fluke.

Whether I'll prove a success in films and so on remains to be seen but I can't keep pulling on the gloves or taping up my knuckles forever. We've all seen the results when fighters stay in the game long after their sell-by date. Great men, brave warriors, reduced to punch-drunk, mumbling old has-beens. I don't want to be that guy.

In June 2016 I would not have classed myself as being famous but my profile was growing, particularly on social media. As a consequence, people had started to hear my name and started looking me up on Facebook, etc. Sure enough, during the build-up to The Guv'nor fight, many positive things started to happen as well, not least getting a part in the Lenny McLean documentary and the bio-pic with Josh Helman. Within a few weeks of signing that contract, Macca and I met Stephen Wood, which led to us working together on this book and securing the book deal with John Blake Publishing. That, though, only came about because we both attended a fund-raiser at Whitehaven for Scott McAvoy's testimonial and that invitation was the result of Alan McDermott's connections and respected status in a rugby-league obsessed part of the county like West Cumbria.

Scott is a fantastic bloke; a local lad who worked his way

through the amateur ranks and went on to captain his local professional team, Whitehaven Rugby League Football Club. Sadly, at his level, these talented athletes and stalwarts of a ferociously hard game retire with very little to show for their years of sacrifice and dedication. So another cracking local lad called Darren Askew, along with lifelong WRLFC supporters like Charles Maudling, organised the fund-raiser. The compere on the night was an old rugby-league rival of Macca's, and now good friend to both of us, Carl Lewthwaite.

The evening was pitched to the punters in the now very familiar and popular 'Audience with' format. The guest speakers were Lenny's son Jamie McLean, Dave Courtney – the former underworld enforcer and host of my very first ever bareknuckle fight – Scott McAvoy and me. Unfortunately, Jamie couldn't make it but the rest of us got up in turn to do a Q&A session with the audience. I followed Courtney. In rugby terms, that's known as a suicide pass because Dave is a natural entertainer and very funny with it, as well as being a very well-connected underworld mover and shaker.

Nevertheless, when my time to speak came, I took the mic and told the story of my past – the bullying, the glue-sniffing, the cocaine, the fighting and self-destructive behaviour – and the room fell silent. Dave Courtney got worried for me and thought I had bombed, bless him. He even chipped in once a twice to liven the room up again but, to be honest, I was comfortable. I could see in the eyes of some that I had touched a nerve. Bullying is something sufferers never forget and, worse, never talk about; a dark, embarrassing episode in their past that they shut away in the recesses of their minds but that never allows them to forget. Depression is also an experience men in particular rarely discuss and yet I saw in the mainly male audience, tell-tale reactions provoked by my honesty.

Naturally, once the Q&A started, most people wanted to know about my life as a fighter and the bareknuckle bouts, about my opponents and my hardest fights. And I was happy to oblige but I'd done what I'd set out to do. I had shown them that even hard and seemingly confident men like me have suffered abuse, bullying and depression and that it's OK to talk about it openly. There is no shame in admitting that the Black Dog sometimes gets the better of you. The shame is that too few people even acknowledge they have a problem for fear of being stigmatised. Depression can be a killer. Intervention might prevent a tragedy happening to someone you love, or even a stranger, if you're alert to the tell-tale signs. It might even be your own life you save. There is always someone willing to listen. Get talking. Get help. Get better. My name is Derek 'Decca' Heggie and I suffer from depression.

Now try this: if you are a sufferer, go and stand in front of a mirror and say out loud to yourself, 'My name is ...and I suffer from depression.' Now go and tell someone else. No, really. Please try it. There is always help. All you have to do is ask. There is always hope. All you have to do is believe. If you don't or can't, don't despair. I guarantee that there is someone out there who does believe in you. Seek them out.

The night went very well and it proved to me that I was on the right path. As a direct result of that Q&A session, Stephen, who knew very little about bareknuckle boxing before we met, contacted Macca and me and asked if I'd ever thought of writing a book about my life story. As it happened, we had but had not actually done much but float the idea. Macca had approached a well-known local author of fiction, who declined, and so, knowing nothing about publishing, we put the idea on the backburner.

Within a couple of weeks of Stephen's call, we'd drawn up an agreement to work together on this book and, by August 2016, had a contract with John Blake Publishing, the very people that published my hero's biography, *The Guv'nor* (aka Lenny McLean). Pinch me, I'm fuckin' dreaming. Oh no, I'm not. If I was, you wouldn't be reading my book.

Another bonus of meeting Carl Lewthwaite was his introduction to Ian Chambers, who owns the Powerhouse Gym at Whitehaven. Ian has been an absolute Godsend: more on him later.

Carl and I formed a good friendship that night and he invited me to another charity night at Whitehaven Rugby League Club. On that occasion, it was a fund-raiser for the Steve Prescott Foundation, which raises funds in support of two brilliant charities: Try Assist and The Christie.

The late, great Steve Prescott MBE was a professional rugby league player for St Helens, a club that has won just about every trophy that code has to offer. He died at the tender age of thirty from a rare form of cancer. His widow, Linzi, and a bunch of other dedicated people now run a charitable foundation in his memory. Despite the poignancy associated with the event, what a cracking night that turned into.

First off, I was introduced to Ade Gardner, a former St Helens and England player; now the club's strength and conditioning coach. Along with him was a Whitehaven lad by the name of Kyle Amor, who now plays for The Saints, and also St Helens winger, Tommy Makinson. Trust me: these boys are proper serious units, tried and tested to the extreme. If ever there was a team sport that is the equivalent of what I do one-to-one, rugby league is that sport. Yes, rugby union is a tough old game as well but tune in and watch a league game if you haven't. It's proper gladiatorial stuff. Every player on the field hits the opposition like a rampaging battering ram, time-after-time for eighty minutes. That's like asking me to go toe-to-toe with Big Dave Price over twenty rounds. Err, no thanks!

These lads are expertly coached and conditioned athletes. They move the ball with speed and precision, sprint and jink, then slam into the opposition at full tilt without coming off the gas. It's a bone-crunching battle of strength and speed; skill and will. No wonder Macca, being an ex-rugby-league player, and I get along so well. The only difference is that, like them, he used to take the opposition on thirteen at a time. Trust me: if you knew Macca, it wouldn't surprise you.

Anyway, on arrival, Carl asked if I wanted to speak. It wasn't scheduled but I said that, if he wanted me to, I would. Despite being sprung upon me out of the blue, it was one of the best talks I have ever given. I saw tears in the eyes of some of the audience and later in the evening a lady approached me to offer her thanks. She said that she had never heard of me before that night but was deeply moved by what I'd said because it touched upon her own story. People like that lady are the reason I talk so openly about my past and the ghosts that still haunt me. Out of my mistakes and experiences, I can help others deal with theirs.

As my notoriety increases (I don't yet think of myself as famous), I've grown increasingly aware and wary of the attention of strangers. Mild paranoia is another downside. I used to welcome friendly attention but, these days, I find myself wondering if some of the people who approach me have an ulterior motive. On the one hand, it makes me feel good that they want to introduce themselves but, on the other hand, it has the negative effect of making me feel a bit of a shit for doubting their sincerity. All too often, though, I have made the mistake of taking some people at face value only to find my association with them came at a price.

It's a minefield. I used to blunder through life without a care in the world. Who was I to worry? I wasn't of any interest to the press or media. Who would be bothered about the antics of a regular lad from Old Harraby who just happens to be handy with his fists? Thankfully, Macca had the foresight to answer that question and had many a long, weary talk with me after I'd done something stupid or made an unguarded remark or posted a rash comment on Facebook. If you ever meet him and wonder why he's bald, he pulled it all out. If you need to know why, look no further. Lesson learned.

The best thing I ever did during my build up to The Guv'nor title fight was close down my Facebook account. At first it felt nearly as bad as when I went cold-turkey off the cocaine because I had become so addicted to chatting with my friends and followers. Within twenty-four hours, though, I had begun to realise how much more relaxed I'd become and how the paranoia had receded. I had deep concerns about the good friends I counsel regarding their depression and not being able to publicise the fight and my merchandise but it was becoming too big a distraction.

It's a great medium for keeping in contact with friends but a terrible means of expressing yourself clearly if, like me, for ease and speed, you tend to use text speak. A simple response can be misinterpreted as a snub, a put down or insult. Before you know it, you're engaged in an all-out slanging match that draws in others from your network. At the click of a mouse, the cyber-bullies round on the accused and rip into them, sometimes with disastrous – even fatal – consequences.

Once bitten, twice shy – shut down! Believe me: I'm still a big fan of Facebook. I'm not one of those people who think that social media should be regulated but I do appeal to its many users to start regulating themselves and to parents to definitely regulate their kids. I've had to. Think about the consequences of what you post because, once it's out there, there is no taking it back.

CHAPTER THIRTEEN

OPPOSITION ALL THE WAY

My Guv'nor title bid was scheduled and cancelled three times before we signed the contract at The Blind Beggar on Wednesday,14 September 2016. That was an eventful day in more ways than one, not least because we finally saw the light at the end of the very long tunnel that had threatened collapse more than once. It was also the day we met the publisher of this book for the first time, John Blake, and his editor. Yet it was one that almost didn't happen, thanks to our piss-poor transport system and London traffic.

The meeting was at Langan's Brasserie in Mayfair. First, though, we had to get there so, once again, before dawn had broken, we were on the M6 and heading for the smoke. It was a horrible drive. Not that I did any driving. We covered endless miles of lane closures owing to roadworks, where nobody actually seemed to be doing any fuckin' work, which, in turn, caused gridlocks and piled misery on the usual commuter hell that is our great British transport system. According to the distance and chosen route, and without breaking any speed limits, we're talking four and a half hours from my house to the hotel in Shoreditch.

Seven bastard hours after setting off, we finally arrived. No time to freshen up or get changed. We had thirty minutes to get from Shoreditch in the east of the capital to Langan's Brasserie in the heart of Mayfair for our first face-to-face with the publisher. It's only about five miles. I could run it in around forty minutes but, in a car in one of the busiest cities in Europe and with a taxi driver who was relying on his sat-nav to get us there, there wasn't a hope in hell that we'd be on time. I've already told you how that meeting went and you're reading the book so no harm done, but would every publisher have been as understanding as John Blake? Top bloke.

We arrived just over an hour late and yet were received with gracious smiles and warm handshakes. What a pair of gents they turned out to be. Langan's is a very plush restaurant in one of London's premier postcodes but those two put us at ease the moment we joined them. No airs and graces, just two professional guys at the top of their game, enjoying a light lunch with a bareknuckle fighter, his dad, his manager and his writer.

Now you might think, 'Yeah, but you're built like a brick shithouse and were about to fight for The Guv'nor title, so what are the odds that a London publisher would get huffy and puffy about being kept waiting by you?' My response to that question is this: John Blake is a very successful publisher – the man responsible for Lenny's bestselling autobiography *The Guv'nor*, as well as Roy Shaw's *Pretty Boy*, to mention but a couple of previous clients from a very long list. What I'm saying is that this particular publisher is quite used to holding face-to-face meetings with hard-men. Not only that, he knows just about every 'face' in the city going back to the latter days of the Krays. As a result, he is not an easy man to impress.

Thankfully, over a delicious lunch, the meeting went really well – so well, in fact, that my editor and I shook hands on a sparring session when I was to return for my pre-fight boot-camp. The young guy had apparently taken up boxing as part of his fitness regime. As we parted, I made a mental note to go easy on the lad come the day. After all, he'd have the last say about what went into the book and what ended on the printing room floor!

Those of you who have followed my career will be aware that, during the build-up to The Guv'nor clash, my opponent was not the man I actually fought for the title. From the day Macca took the call offering me a shot at the vacant title, right up until a month before the showdown, my official opponent was a London hard-man of Welsh origin, Phil Davis (or Welsh Phil, as he's known down the smoke). So how come I ended up taking on that man-mountain and ex-pro heavyweight Julius Francis? The reasons are as complex as they are numerous but it boiled down to Welsh Phil having health problems, and objections from the Metropolitan Police.

For the record, let me state loud and clear that Welsh Phil was up for it from day one. Despite our differences, Phil did not bottle it; he reluctantly withdrew on grounds of ill health and police harassment of the organisers. I don't know, nor want to know, what beef the Met have with Phil but I do want the readers of my book to know that this man was more than willing to take me on. If you doubt that, just watch him on

YouTube when he went mental in the ring at my appearance in the crowd at Crystal Palace where he was fighting. After watching that clip, ask yourself: does that look like a man who was scared of facing me in the ring?

Furthermore, some critics reckoned Phil wasn't a credible opponent. Really? They cited such things as our size and weight differential. In reply to that, I give you Roy Shaw's victory over Lenny McLean in their first showdown. Roy gave away a lot more height and weight to Lenny than Phil would have against me. The Guv'nor fight isn't like a sanctioned British Board of Boxing Control fight. It's arranged according to the traditions of pitting hard-men against each other by promoters who know that scene. Previous holders have come in all sorts of shapes and sizes and the title only became vacant after the tragic death of Joe Katts in a motorcycle accident.

The title came from the tradition of holding 'straighteners' between neighbourhood enforcers, who were known as Guv'nors, to see who would emerge as guv'nor of guv'nors. Back in the day, all the rougher districts of London were ruled by their local guv'nor. Lenny McLean, for instance, took over from whoever was the guv'nor in the Hoxton area of the East End and, of course, as his reputation grew as a hard-man, so his influence spread into other districts. When there was trouble on their manor, the police were rarely called for.

The police did what they could to enforce the law but the 'sorting out' of low-level stuff and domestic disputes was generally left to the neighbourhood guv'nor. If someone was taking liberties – maybe nicking off his own neighbours or bullying a neighbour – the guv'nor would get to hear about it and the miscreant would get sorted out. Of course, there was always another up-and-coming guv'nor waiting in the wings to dethrone the incumbent or inherit his mantle when old age eventually took its toll but the sitting guv'nor enjoyed great respect on his manor.

Eventually, some bright spark came up with the idea of having them fight it out to see who came out on top and The Guv'nor title was born. Size didn't, and still doesn't, come into it where Guv'nor bouts are concerned. If you were hard enough and willing to meet all challengers, you could claim the title. Let me give you an example from up our way. There's a bit of a legendary character from Maryport, a fishing port in the west of Cumbria, called Charlie Rundle. He's knocking on a bit now and retired; a quiet unassuming gent by all reports. Not only that, Charlie's a modest man who'll probably be embarrassed by my bigging him up but credit where credit's due.

Charlie wasn't, and would never have claimed to be, the guv'nor of that town but, in his day, he was a man who other hard-men around that town rated and respected. In his prime, Charlie weighed in at a slim twelve and a half stone and yet he could wipe the floor with much bigger fellers but he wasn't a dirty fighter. In his heyday, he scythed through quite a few big, hard blokes, with lighting-sharp, killer punches, because they made the same mistake some of you reading this book will probably make. People equate size with power but fighting prowess comes from deep within. Courage is something you cannot build in a gym.

One scalp of the many he claimed was that of a very well-known Carlisle hard-case, now deceased, who I shan't name out of respect for his memory. He made the mistake of going to Maryport on Carnival Day and then picking a quarrel with Charlie. That old saying 'It's not the size of the dog in the fight but the fight in the dog that counts' really applied where the dapper Charlie was concerned. Not one for putting on a show, Charlie invited him to 'take a walk' with him up the fields. A short time later, only Charlie returned to rejoin the festivities and his much bigger challenger never ever attended the Maryport Carnival again.

Long before it became apparent that Phil was having kidney trouble, rumours abounded of a clash at the proposed venue between his tasty firm, backed up by his Welsh supporters, and the boys from Carlisle who planned to travel down *en masse* to support me. Carlisle and Cardiff share an enmity that goes back to the football-hooligan years of the late 1970s and the 1980s. The police feared a pitched battle at the venue incited by the English-Welsh rivalry in the ring. It was all bollocks, of course, but was enough for the Met to say, 'No, not on our turf – not ever!' My camp was convinced it was being stoked by petty jealousy.

Rival promoters and shadier characters in the BKB network did not want Decca Heggie fighting for Lenny's coveted belt and definitely didn't want me to win the title. Why? You'd have to ask them. What was happening, though, was that a venue would be arranged and, within a short space of time, withdrawn because they'd received anonymous calls warning of trouble. On another occasion, it was because the fight had been billed on social media as 'the biggest gangland fight since Lenny McLean took on Roy Shaw.'

It was never a gangland fight. I'm not a gangster, nor have I ever run with gangsters. I had that one fight in Dave Courtney's back garden and even he doesn't claim to be a gangster. He was primarily a debt-collector and ran a large door-security firm. Yes, he's been a very naughty geezer and is well known as a 'celebrity gangster' but it's not a tag he likes or chose. That fight in his garden is as close as I have come to 'hanging with gangsters.' Even then, Dave took me to one side and, after congratulating me over my victory, he gave me a piece of sound advice. He said, 'If you want to succeed at this game, Decca, stay away from me and guys like me. All we do is attract police attention.'

I thought that was proper decent of him, having hosted the event and been impressed by my performance. That's Dave though. I was told that he's a genuine fella who puts other people before himself and that proved it. Having witnessed the birth of a natural bareknuckle talent, others might have kept me close and cashed in, and did, but not him. And based on what went on in the build-up to the fight, his words proved absolutely true. The word 'gangland' appearing on the social media had the Metropolitan Police straight on the blower to Ricky English.

You might well ask: why then hold press conferences and conduct signings at The Blind Beggar? That venue is synonymous with the gangster scene of the 1960s and the very pub in which Ronnie Kray shot and killed George Cornell. The short answer is: I don't really know. These days it's a tourist attraction as much as anything else and definitely not the haunt of underworld figures. Why would gangsters want to hang out in a pub that is full of people taking pictures and selfies?

Signing up fighters and posing outside The Blind Beggar has simply become a tradition at that venue. Fighters and promoters paying homage to the ghosts of the past, in the East End of London, where the roots of all previous Guv'nor fights first took hold.

I took heed of Dave's advice and ever since have tried

not to get drawn into the darker side of the BKB world. Perhaps that's the reason I've made enemies with some from that scene. Whether they are the real deal or not, quite a few like to think they're gangsters, or at least act the part. Christian Roberts, for instance, but he was definitely of the plastic variety. Yes, I have met some and, on two occasions only, collected the purse I was due thanks to their presence but that's what happens when you fight on the unlicensed and bareknuckle circuits. It's a sport that draws them, just as professional boxing does.

Whatever was behind it, as a consequence of all this interference, every time Ricky and Joey Jnr got it set up, a protest would be lodged, a whispering campaign launched and the Met would get involved and that would see those plans scuppered. Those two guys must have lost hundreds of pounds having tickets and flyers printed, only to bin the lot within a few days of receiving them. I know Macca was at the end of his tether having arranged and cancelled travel plans, hotel bookings and the like on at least three occasions.

During the protracted negotiations, concerns had been raised that Welsh Phil was not as fit as he looked. He'd lost a lot of weight. That was put down to a rigorous pre-fight conditioning programme. When pressed, though, the tough fucker finally coughed to having 'a bit of kidney trouble.' This feller was going to get in the ring with me and it turned out he needed kidney surgery. I might have killed him but he tried his level best to mask the problem, rather than be seen as dodging the fight. So don't you ever doubt Welsh Phil's courage or credentials. He's a fighting man and he'll be back.

Into the breach stepped the colossal Julius Francis. Now *I* had a problem. I'd been preparing to take on a much lighter and very mobile unlicensed fighter. Suddenly, I was faced with a towering hulk and ex-pro with a raft of titles to his name, which included a coveted Lonsdale Belt. Weeks of training and studying videos to develop tactics to get around Welsh Phil's furious, all-out aggression and through his defences was, all of a sudden, out of the window. Julius presented an altogether different style of fighter and a much, much bigger problem.

The man might have been less mobile and past his heavy-weight prime but make no mistake: he was still more than capable of pounding an opponent into submission. He wasn't exactly ring-rusty either, being particularly active in bringing youngsters on in the sport.

My detractors forget that I had never had a professional boxing match, having only fought on the unlicensed and BKB circuits. In my eyes, against Julius Francis I was the underdog but not if you were to believe the snipers and character assassins on social media. They were slating a man who had fought the likes of Danny Williams, Scott Welch, Michael Holden, Sinan Samil Sam, Vitali Klitchko and Mike Tyson. Somehow, in their twisted world, Julius Francis vs Decca Heggie was a poor match. Are they seriously putting me up there with Big Bad Mike? I'd be flattered if it wasn't so insane. However, when you consider that those same critics thought Welsh Phil was an unsuitable contender, you are left to conclude that there is no pleasing some people.

Overnight I'd gone from facing a London-Welsh wild-man to a seasoned ex-pro with over forty-eight fights; a man who had faced four future world-heavyweight title holders. Granted he hadn't beaten any of the future champions but, with my lack of professional experience and raw, street-fighting style,

I doubt I would have either. People like Julius know how to take the edge off a good shot and, when they can't, they have the experience to ride one long enough to recover and counter. Seasoned veterans like Julius can appear to be doing very little as they pick their way through their opponent's defences with power and precision. Believe you me: the guy on the receiving end is all too painfully aware of what is happening.

Julius's manager, Teddy Bam-Bam, is a long-time associate and friend of Joey Pyle Jnr. Teddy's what you might call a colourful character. He runs a tasty London security firm, R-Knights, of which Julius is his head doorman. When it became apparent Welsh Phil could not fight, Joey Jnr sounded out his mate Teddy about big Julius's availability and willingness to get into the ring with me. From what I can gather, Julius didn't think twice. Does that sound like the response of a fighter who's over the hill? He clearly didn't think so.

The next thing you know, I'm up against a guy who holds multiple heavyweight titles and a Lonsdale belt. Not only does Julius keep his hand in around a boxing gym, he is regularly called upon to deal with fights on the dance floors and doors. So let's have no more talk about Julius being past it when we fought. If you truly think that, take him on yourself and see if you can stay on your feet under that pile-driver jab.

Trust me: when he walked into the beer garden at The Blind Beggar, it suddenly went dark. Julius Francis is one big unit with an equally big and confident smile. Yes, I signed up for the fight and, like Welsh Phil, I wasn't going to make any excuses but one thing was sure: I had to get back to the gym, and fast. I was giving away height, four and a half stone in weight and reach, and the gulf in experience was as wide as the Grand Canyon. This opponent meant getting back to basics and drawing up a whole new fight strategy.

Out of the on-off mayhem emerged an event that combined my fight for The Guv'nor title with adaptive boxing under the banner of my good friend Colin Wood's Adaptive Boxing Organisation (ABO). My journey from unlicensed boxing through bareknuckle fighting to The Guv'nor had come full circle. Colin had taken me under his wing after the Bulldog fight and here we were, reunited on the night my dream came true.

The ABO was set up by Colin Wood to offer willing and enthusiastic able and adaptive athletes the opportunity to compete in boxing tournaments. He had put in place coaching to develop the skills of those with previous experience and to bring on novices. The main aim of the organisation is to foster confidence and self-belief in people born with, or those who have suffered, life-changing physical impairment. Many of these men and women have previously engaged in martial arts and eagerly accepted the challenge of retraining to compete, despite the restrictions their condition imposes. Others are entering the sport for the very first time.

Before you criticise Colin for encouraging them, consider this: these people are fighters in every sense of the word. Every day is a fight for them and being afforded the chance to express themselves in a physical challenge beyond that which they face daily provides a great boost to their self-esteem, confidence and their zest for life. If you think what I do is hard, just spend a day in the company of some of these incredible people and then tell me what Colin is doing for them is wrong. Not only have they learned to live with their condition but they have overcome the restrictions it places on them by never accepting defeat. They are the very definition of fighters and, if, like able-bodied athletes do, they want to test themselves against each other, who are we to deny them that opportunity?

These athletes face enough obstacles without well-meaning, able-bodied people placing further restrictions on their lives and lifestyle choices. Along the way Colin has courted controversy and has had to battle prejudice and misguided accusations of exploitation in order to secure a future for the sport and the athletes who choose to participate. As an engineer, Colin did not take on this challenge lightly. A great deal of time spent in consultation and research has gone into creating the right equipment to enable the adaptive combatants to engage in a sport they love, on equal terms and in a safe and controlled environment.

They are to be admired and not looked upon as curiosities. What they do is so much harder than anything I have to face. The success of the Paralympics and Invictus Games that Prince Harry set up are testament to the desire disabled and adaptive athletes have to engage in competitive sports and I see adaptive boxing as an extension of that ethos. Critics of boxing will no doubt look upon adaptive boxing as a gross distortion of an already unjustifiable activity. That argument has raged since pugilism became a recognised sport. But we fighters are responding to something primal in human nature and accept the risks that come with our sport.

Ours is not the only sport to carry risks of serious injury, even death. In fact, many sports, particularly motorsports, have a much higher casualty rate than boxing and have certainly accounted for more deaths in the pursuit of victory. *But*, even as we worked on this book, British welterweight

Mike Towell tragically died from his injuries in a title fight in Glasgow – the first to do so since the sport lost James Murray and Jimmy Garcia in 1995. Death in the ring is a real and constant threat that cannot be ignored and quite naturally attracts criticism.

Any death in the pursuit of sporting achievement seems unnecessary – avoidable even – but only if human beings decide to stop risking their lives in pursuit of their chosen sports, their goals and their dreams. The evidence suggests that, despite the risks and the losses, people will always compete in dangerous and combative sports. It's in our nature. And boxing remains enormously popular. My heart goes out to Mike Towell's family and friends and to Dale Evans, his opponent that night. He will be suffering too.

Boxing will always get bad press because two people stand face-to-face and slug it out but look at how many other sports put the human body through unimaginable pain that even result in death and nobody bats an eye-lid. How many mountaineers and rock climbers die every year? I tell you something: I'd rather go ten rounds with another heavyweight any day of the week than drag my arse up Everest wondering all the way if I'll ever reach the summit and, if I do, whether I'll get back down again. A lot don't and some that do lose fingers, toes and even the tips of their noses to frostbite. Apart from the professional guides and local Sherpas, the bulk of folk who go up there aren't even getting paid for risking their lives. What the fuck's that about?

I'd be willing to bet that quite a few of these people who pursue potentially fatal 'sporting activities' are among those who think that boxing and other combat sports, such as MMA and so on, should be banned because they pose a risk to the competitors' health and, on rare occasions, result in serious and life-changing injuries. In the whole history of boxing, though, deaths during a bout are very rare indeed.

The bottom line is this: some people just like to fight; others to run, swim, climb or jump. Each one is an activity developed from our ancient and basic need to survive. Whether it's on the track, in a pool, on a pitch or in a ring, some people will always follow that urge to test themselves against others or the environment and physical impairment doesn't necessarily diminish those primal instincts. Don't criticise my friend Colin for encouraging and facilitating disabled and adaptive athletes – applaud him. Better still: applaud the participants for their dedication, determination and unquestionable courage.

CHAPTER FOURTEEN

LIGHTS, CAMERA, ACTION

Although Eamonn O'Keefe was the first film director to float the idea of me appearing in a film, my actual debut was a part in my dream movie, *My Name Is Lenny*, a biopic about the early days in the life of my hero, Lenny McLean. The film was to open with my character fighting The Guv'nor, Lenny McLean, played by the Australian actor, Josh Helman. In a truly ironic twist, I was cast as one of Lenny's arch-rivals, Blockie Johnson, and I had to fight Josh, as Lenny, 'on the cobbles', on location in an East End back street. Just over a month after filming that scene, I was in a boxing ring at the Clapham Grand fighting Julius Francis for The Guv'nor title. Talk about art imitating life.

How did it happen that an unlicensed boxer and bareknuckle fighter landed a part in a major film that also boasted the great Sir John Hurt in its cast list along with Josh Helman in the lead role? Well, believe it or not, I was talent spotted at my last bareknuckle fight in that cesspit in Pontefract when I made short work of Clifford Gray to win the Heavyweight Pit Fighting Belt – that's how. To think that we very nearly gave it up as a bad job and got back in the car. Had we done so, I might never have got my first shot at film acting.

Jamie McLean, Lenny's son, was making a documentary about his dad and had attended the Clifford Gray fight to shoot some footage. After he'd watched me demolish Clifford in double-quick time, he asked if I'd be interested in a small part in a forthcoming movie about his dad. Interested? I was fuckin' ecstatic but never imagined it would actually happen. Believe me: fighting on the BKB circuit does tend to make you deeply cynical. I've had all sorts of offers that turned out to be a load of bollocks. On face value, this sounded too good to be true and so experience told me that it probably was. There was something about Jamie, though. His approach wasn't accompanied by all the usual nudge-nudge, wink-wink, nose-tapping bullshit.

Jamie's the real deal. He's been there. Fighting is in his blood. From a very early age he had seen his dad come home bearing cuts and bruises from his many battles on the cobbles and in the ring, at gypsy fairs and on the doors of London's nightclubs. When he clocked me at Pontefract, Jamie knew what he was looking at: the kind of fighter his dad would have relished going toe-to-toe with. Better still, with the chiselled good looks of a matinee idol. *What?* OK then, the kind of broad-shouldered, hard-bastard Ron needed for his big opening scene.

It was one of those 'pinch me, I must be dreaming' moments when Jamie tapped me up at the fight but it didn't take him long to confirm his offer. A short time after that fight, Jamie got back in touch and invited me down to the 'wrap party' for the documentary at The Blind Beggar and, from there, to its premiere at the Genesis cinema, just down the road from that infamous pub. It was at the party that I was first introduced to the film's director, Ron Scalpello, and he seemed just as enthusiastic about casting me in the part of Blockie Johnson. After the premiere we talked some more and Ron invited me down to work with his stunt team on the crucial fight scene that was to open his movie.

When we got talking at The Blind Beggar and after the premiere, it was obvious that Ron had a clear vision of the impact he wanted his opening scene to have on its audience. I got all excited just listening to him as he explained how the action would unfold. I don't know how much fighting he's done or watched but he obviously knows his way around a scrap and I instinctively knew I could deliver a very convincing fight scene. We shook hands on it and, provided I did the business at the rehearsals, I was on the cast list.

On that subject, another name that jumped straight out at me when I eventually saw the cast list was that of Rita Tushingham, who has starred in over thirty films, alongside countless TV and theatre appearances. Then there was UFC legend turned actor Michael Bisping, who played Roy Shaw. So they had cast two professional fighters and hard-men, me and Michael, to play two infamous fighters and hard-bastards. I knew straight away that Ron and Paul were very serious about making their film feel as authentic as they possibly could. Not only was I going to enjoy the experience, I knew I was taking part in a film I would have gone to see and eventually added to my DVD collection anyway.

Ron Scalpello began his working life as a young music

journalist and writing for *Goal* magazine, which I picked off the shelves in the newsagents as a football-crazy kid. After that he moved into making award-winning music videos, promos and commercials, which is how Sir Ridley Scott and one or two other great directors got started. So Ron's treading a familiar and successful path to success and, who knows: the Oscars maybe. Going by my limited experience, I reckon he's definitely got the talent to rake in awards.

His chance to move into directing mainstream films came with *Offender*, starring Joe Cole and written by his producer for *My Name Is Lenny*, Paul Van Carter. That film was quickly followed by *Pressure*, starring Danny Huston, Matthew Goode and Joe Cole, and early 2017 saw the premiere of the film in which I made my acting debut. Cheers, Ron. Thank you for the opportunity and for placing your trust in a complete acting novice. OK, so as a winner-takes-all street-fighter, I was typecast but there's a lot more to filming a convincing fight scene than fake blood, grunting at the right moment and throwing a few air-shots.

With an up-and-coming young star like Josh Helman playing the young Lenny and big names from the industry like the (sadly, late) Sir John Hurt in the cast, I knew I was getting my acting break in what could become a big hit and I couldn't wait to get started. What a break it turned out to be too. Actually, I've got ahead of myself again here. When I was first approached by Jamie and then offered the part by Ron, they had Sir Michael Gambon cast in the role John Hurt eventually played but the poor fella injured himself filming in Canada and had to withdraw. Sir Michael, Sir John, it was all the same to me. I was going to be in a film with a mega-star.

The small but crucial part I played meant I didn't actually

get to work with John Hurt or Rita Tushingham but the whole crew and cast could not have been more welcoming and supportive, and none more so than the film's star, Josh Helman, who had appeared in *Mad Max: Fury Road* and two X-Men movies, among others. I don't mind telling you I was a quite nervous and star-struck to begin with. As it turned out, I needn't have been.

Some of them were no less in awe of what I do for a living. Josh himself was one. Being such a good actor, he proved a very convincing hard-man and fighter but, knowing that I did that sort of shit for a living, he showed me great respect throughout. I learned so much working through the scene and acting opposite him in rehearsals and on the day of the shoot. Somehow Josh morphed from an easy-going, Australian heart-throb and action-hero into the East End's most notorious and respected hard-man before my very eyes. But it was during the day of rehearsals that we first gelled as actors and, by the end of the day, good mates. He still keeps in touch.

Ron Scalpello wasn't anything like I'd expected. Not at all arty-farty; he's a real down-to-earth bloke who comes across as a bit of a geezer but the guy is proper switched on and obviously knows his stuff. What impressed me most, though, when we eventually did get down to work, was his relaxed and easy way with the cast, crew and technicians. Make no mistake: he was in charge and knew what he wanted but he wasn't at all loud or rude. He just quietly got on with the job, occasionally stepping in to offer guidance and advice while, at the same time, he proved perfectly willing to listen to someone else's point of view. This was never better demonstrated than when I first stepped in front of the cameras at 3 Mills Studios, not far from West Ham Football Club's old ground.

Macca and I had set off from Carlisle at 'What-the-fuck? o'clock' and got to the studios just before 1pm. Jamie, Ron, Josh, Paul Van Carter, the stunt co-ordinator, Tony Lucken and two of his team, Josh's stunt-double, David Chapman and Charlie Siveyer and the technicians were already busy working out camera angles and the fight choreography but stopped what they were doing the moment we appeared. The weirdest thing is that I was more nervous about taking part in a pretend fight than I have ever been facing a genuine and dangerous opponent. Such is the effect that movie cameras and a little stardust can have.

Straight away they all put me at my ease before Ron got down to explaining what was required of me: a realistic straightener between two hard men. Piece of piss! Then the head of make-up got her hands on me – literally. Sue, a very bubbly South African lady, sat me down to figure out how she would set about transforming me into a convincing 1970s London tough-guy. No problem, provided I didn't shave off the beard or moustache before filming commenced. I had no plans to, so Sue was happy enough.

In no time, Ron put me to work with Tony and his two stuntmen, David and Charlie. First things first: I had to learn the moves. David and Charlie demonstrated every blow, grapple, recoil and fall with me right alongside Charlie shadowing his every move. Then Charlie stepped aside and I took over. Tony and his team had been working on this sequence for weeks and, thanks to my years of street-fighting experience, I soon had it down. Creating a seven-minute fight scene, however, involves an awful lot of repetition as the director works out the best angles from which to shoot it to the best effect. So we went over and over the routine until it was imprinted in my memory and the moves became second nature.

After several takes, my confidence had begun to grow and one or two doubts had started to creep into my head. They might have been experts in what they do but I was the expert in the room when it came to street-fighting and elements of the fight choreography just didn't ring true. Eventually, and to the surprise of everyone, I called a halt. Quite politely, I explained that I had been in many a street-fight and that, at the critical point, when Blockie stepped over the mark, which caused Lenny to go absolutely ape-shit and smash the poor fucker to bits, they were getting it wrong.

Ron asked me to demonstrate what I meant and so I asked David, Josh's stunt double, to assume the position over me after Lenny has knocked Blockie to the ground. I got down and told David to act out what he we had been rehearsing as Lenny (David) reached down to help Blockie (me) to his feet while congratulating him on a good fight. That was Lenny's mind-set at that point, you see. Blockie was down if not quite out. Job done, fight over, purse won, help the beaten opponent up and no hard feelings.

This time, though, so as to give David a chance to react and to best demonstrate how a real street-fighter would take advantage in that situation, as I sprung up, but in slow-motion, I feigned a reverse head-butt, bringing the back of my head up into his jaw. It's a move that would throw an unwary opponent off balance. As Lenny (David) reacted, as any man would, by instinctively recoiling and taking a step back, I lunged and aimed a proper head-butt at his face, which didn't connect, of course, then stopped and turned to Ron and the crew.

'That's what *would* happen in a street fight. Trust me: I've had quite a few.' I explained with a cheeky grin.

Ron loved that piece of improvisation and asked that we do it again but this time at more normal speed and it worked beautifully. That unexpected and illegal move, in what was supposed to be a fist-fight, would be a more credible trigger to Lenny's rage, which is how the script described the fight's climax, and that was what had been bugging me. The way it was written, with Blockie just getting up and engaging him again, wouldn't have caused the fight to degenerate into a brutal all-out assault that resulted in Lenny almost killing Blockie with a blitz of punches before stomping him into the cobbles. What had been lacking until then was a believable trigger moment that would have tipped Lenny over the edge into a blind fury and I had come up with one.

After running through it a couple of times at full-speed, Ron rewrote that section of the fight scene to include my improvisation. I was absolutely chuffed to bits. Then it was time for Josh to step up and go through the whole scene with me again. The fight involved a complex series of moves that Josh had been practising as well and, like the skilled professional he is, he was very good but it still didn't feel real enough. So once again I made a suggestion.

During one of the clinches as Blockie (me) grappled with Lenny (Josh), I said, 'Hit me.' Josh looked shocked. 'Go on, hit me. Don't worry, you won't hurt me,' I encouraged. 'I've been hit by much bigger fellas than you, mate.'

So Josh started landing a few shots on my arms and torso. The lad doesn't lack power but it wasn't anything I couldn't handle and it made for a much more realistic fight scene. Josh, Ron and the crew were blown away by my willingness to let him actually strike as opposed to throw air-shots. With the scene working well as we worked through the routine, I began to ad-lib Blockie's verbal responses as well. That really tickled them 'cause I can do a fairly passable Cockney accent: 'McLean, you fuckin' mug. I ain't done yet,' and stuff like that. I started snarling as we exchanged blows, him landing a few as I had suggested but all of mine convincing air-shots. Throw in a few sound effects, a bit of verbal and, by the magic of the movies, you have a totally believable fight. I absolutely loved the whole experience and was hooked. This just might be the career path I can follow after I finally give up the fight game.

By the end of the day I was not only a big fan but had found a new friend in Josh Helman. He posed for photographs with us and even sent a nice text message to Macca's daughter wishing her well for her forthcoming wedding. As for Ron Scalpello and Paul Van Carter, they were over the moon because, having learned my part so quickly, I'd saved them around five hours work, which amounted to quite a saving on the tight budget.

We headed home with me on an absolute high and looking forward to the day of the actual shoot. Paul had even asked Macca if he fancied being an extra, as the fight scene would involve a baying crowd of supporters from both sides and gamblers betting on the outcome. You know he couldn't resist, don't you!

Between the rehearsals and the actual shoot I got down to some serious training. Of course, at that time I was still preparing to face Welsh Phil Davis and so was not only concentrating on stamina but studying his fights to look for a way through his frenetic, aggressive style. To be perfectly honest, Phil doesn't really do defence. He's an all-out attack dog. Not so much 'Raging Bull' – more like snarling pitbull.

I'd upped my distance a little on my runs and, as I said earlier to make it even harder, I would do the first three or four miles wearing an altitude-training mask that simulates running at 9,000 feet. With that clamped to my face, three miles felt like nine and I'd get the strangest looks as I jogged around the roads and lanes.

By this time, I was regularly stopping at Stephen and his wife Sue's place to work with him on the book. I'm not usually comfortable under a strange roof but their house quickly became a real home from home. So much so that I really began to look forward to my visits, to Sue's home cooking and to snuggling with their two lovely dogs, Fitz and Gryff. I was stopping with them when they lost the older dog, Fitz, and I don't mind telling you I shed a few tears as I shared in the grief. I had become so attached to Fitz; he used to lie beside me and rest his head in my lap.

Knowing I was keen to stick with my regimen, Stephen introduced me to a gruelling little six-mile run that involved a few long and fairly steep climbs. The first couple of times I really struggled but, as my stamina improved, I was even finishing the last 150-metre uphill stretch at a decent pace.

I would combine my visits with training at Chem's Powerhouse Gym in Whitehaven and, yes, I'd drag my writer along. If he was going to make me slave over this fuckin' book, I was going to have him feel the burn at the gym – and he did! On other occasions we'd go into Workington, where I got to know a few notorious locals, like Robbo, who has since proved a really good friend. It was Robbo that set up the boxing lessons I had with Mark Hodgson at his Hokushinko

Fight Academy. Stephen drew the line at sparring. He's not as stupid as he looks! Mark's a sixth dan in Karate Wado-Kai with thirty-plus years of experience but is pretty much an expert in most forms of martial arts, including boxing.

In no time at all, he'd developed a strategy to deal with Welsh Phil's full-on-barrage style and I was feeling very confident. Then word came through that Welsh Phil had had to pullout and so those tactics I'd been learning were of no more use. Phil's replacement, Julius Francis, demanded a complete rethink and Mark got straight on the case.

The movie business: what can I tell you? All high-living, red-carpet treatment and glamour... *not!* I was required in make-up at 6.30am. Fair enough, they sent a car for us. It picked us up at the hotel door and deposited us around the corner at the shoot's operational base in Emma Street. I shit you not. I don't think we travelled more than 200 metres. So at that time, I was beginning to believe the film business was a life of ridiculous excess and pampering, until we joined the crew in what looked like a disused depot of some kind. We were greeted warmly by Ron's third assistant director, Rory Broadfoot, and told to grab some breakfast before everyone else arrived.

Oh yeah, full English, if that's was your fancy, all sorts of cereals, yoghurt, fruit, fruit juice and hot drinks galore but there was no escaping the fact we were in an old loading bay in the East End. Glamorous it wasn't. There was a huge mobile make-up van where my South African friend, Sue, waited eagerly with razors, wigs and face paint. Josh Helman turned up in a black hoodie and matching baseball cap at around 7am and just mingled in with everyone else. No starry 'leading-man' attitude. After acknowledging everyone, he homed in on the stuntmen, clearly concerned that they'd get the job done and that he and they would deliver the best performance they could.

A tarp-covered frame housed the costumes in which we all got kitted out and a rapidly growing throng of assistants, extras and technicians assembled. It was organised chaos but, somehow, out of it, a bunch of dodgy-looking geezers dressed in 1970s garb emerged – none more dodgy-looking than Macca. The icing on the cake of his outfit came later: a tan suede trilby to crown the ginger, out-sized mutton-chop sideburns make-up he had glued to his face. He looked like *Emmerdale Farm*'s, Seth Armstrong's illegitimate son after a one-night stand with Pat Butcher from *EastEnders* round the back of the Old Vic – or was it the Woolpack? We fuckin' howled.

Before long, we were bundled into a vehicle and driven to Ezra Street, where the fight scene was to be shot. The producers had secured the area and we'd got the 'L'-shaped cobbled back-street all to ourselves for the day while Ron Scalpello worked his magic. The first thing I noticed was a bike hoisted and tied off at the top of a streetlight. These are the sorts of details we don't think about. Some local had locked his bike to that lamppost for security reasons but it wasn't in keeping with the era so it had to be out of the shot.

The crew couldn't cut the lock off; that would be criminal damage. Instead, they used their initiative and lifted the bike right to the top of the street light and, because they couldn't get it over the top, tied it off. And that is where it stayed for the whole day. There's a degree of inconvenience when shooting a film in anyone's neighbourhood but, in the main, almost everyone accepted it, bar a snooty twat on his pushbike who thought the hundred-metre detour most unreasonable and a pair of ladies who accused the security man and the rest of us of being racists! To my knowledge, the poor bloke had merely pointed out that, while filming, access to Ezra Street was restricted.

Josh turned up with Charley Palmer Rothwell, who played Carrots McLean. It was incredible watching Josh, as Lenny, strut up that street past the period Jensen Interceptor parked beside the old pub they had to enter before Ron called 'cut'. His walk, mannerisms, facial twitches and jutting jaw were so evocative of my childhood hero. Watch the film and then watch some of the old footage on YouTube of Lenny and you'll see what I mean. He's a dead-ringer.

Then they called us to the corner to set up the fight scene. Well, I've had hard fights but I'm telling you, none of them proved as hard or exhausting as the pretend scrap I had to engage in that day – over and over again. The longer the day wore on, the harder it got. We'd got lucky and found ourselves filming on a virtually cloudless day but it was one of the hottest September days on record for years. We were all pissing with sweat as we went through the routine repeatedly so that Ron could shoot the sequence from several different angles.

We'd shoot close-ups into the camera then with crowd noise, then without crowd noise, then with Josh speaking his lines and me ad-libbing mine, then with Josh singing a song to the mob as Blockie writhes in agony on the cobbles. By the time Ron called 'a wrap', we were all absolutely knackered. I looked like I'd been through an abattoir. Honestly, I've never shed so much blood in all my fights put together. Granted, this was all fake but, fuckin' hell, Lenny must have given Blockie one hell of a hammering. I felt pretty beaten up as well.

The scene called for me to get knocked down a couple of times but I was dropping onto cobbles. Sometimes there was a mat there, sometimes not, because they would be shooting the scene with an overhead camera or in close-up. On those occasions, I had to drop onto those worn cobbles, which had withstood years of traffic, so Decca Heggie wasn't likely to make much of an impression on them but they did on me.

Then, of course, Josh was landing those shots I'd told him to follow through with for the sake of realism. The trouble is that, after six hours of repeatedly being pounded on the arms and shoulders, and of being stamped on, my arms – the tools of my trade – were fairly sore. Josh had followed through a little too convincingly with the heel of his shoe quite few times towards the end of the day and caught me in the knackers once but I just sucked it up because they were rolling. The cameras! Not my knackers. It's a technical expression. Oh, and my ribs felt like he'd been playing a tune on them with a mallet. Otherwise, I was just fine. Very tired and a little dehydrated but I wouldn't have missed it for the world.

After Ron called proceedings to a halt, he gathered the crew around and personally thanked me for my contribution. It was a really nice gesture, I thought, and quite humbling. Ron even told me that he'd keep me in mind for a couple of other projects he was considering. I'd arrived that morning quietly confident that I could deliver the performance he was looking for but never imagined I would make such a good impression. After a few photo-ops and selfies, it was time to get cleaned up and get the hell out of London. No disrespect to you Londoners reading this but give me Carlisle any day of the week.

On the long drive home I slept quite a lot of the time and

that bought Macca and Stephen time to plot a proper piss-take. I woke up well north of the capital and Macca told me that Ron had been discussing his next film project with him. Stephen immediately concurred. That caught my attention. I knew I'd done the business but wasn't expecting another offer so soon after my debut.

'Yeah, he's filming a sort of British version of *Brokeback Mountain*,' Macca explained, in all seriousness.

'Aye, two lonely shepherds stuck on a lonely fell,' Stephen added. Suddenly, the weariness cleared. 'Don't worry, the graphic-sex scenes will be simulated,' he said.

'Oh yeah, you just have to get naked with another guy and do a bit of snogging is all, mate,' Macca chipped in.

'Apart from that one scene,' said Stephen pointedly. 'The close-up. Ron really wants to see you chug on that thrusting bad boy.'

By this time I knew it was a wind-up. 'What is this? Take the piss out of Decca day? 'I asked, settling back down.

They kept it up for a while and even Dad joined in but I didn't mind. It had been one hell of a day and one I'll never forget. My first appearance on the big screen was but a few months away and I was feeling pretty fuckin' chuffed.

CHAPTER FIFTEEN

BAD BLOOD AND BAD TIMING

If you have watched any of the videos of Welsh Phil Davis on YouTube, you might have concluded that he's a bit of an animal. He certainly doesn't hold back or mince his words. He had a lot to say about me and none of it very flattering. It doesn't bother or impress me and, as for dissing the opposition, that's just not my style – sticks and stones. In reply, I posted a polite but pointed response, which is also available to view on YouTube.

In truth, I don't know Welsh Phil; we've only met the one time, at Crystal Palace. A record of that encounter is on that same website for all to see. To be fair, my being there might be seen by many as a provocation that, in turn, triggered his OTT reaction but all fighters do these things. It's all part of the fun and games; the circus show that has become a pre-fight build-up tradition. We meet in order to ratchet up the tension and, hopefully, boost ticket sales. Just as I met with Julius Francis at The Blind Beggar, it's all part and parcel of the sport. Julius is an old pro and a much more laid-back character than Welsh Phil: he greeted the sight of me with a friendly smile and a handshake. Of course, we also posed with fists raised for the cameras, as is expected.

After saying all that, I still reserve the right not to pass judgement on Phil based on one meeting and his ranting about me on social media. Yes, he came across as a bit crazy but was it an act? Was he performing for the cameras? Perhaps his 'hold me back' rabid-dog routine was just him doing his bit to drum up publicity for the fight but in his own inimitable style. Or is he really some kind of raving maniac who genuinely doesn't rate me? The jury is out.

Depending on how his recovery from his kidney trouble goes and what the public and promoters want, we may never know. All I can say is that, as long as I continue to fight for a living, I won't dodge Welsh Phil. Nor do I believe that he will avoid any future fight that might be arranged. He's been there and won the belt before, so he knows what it takes. I hardly think he would have agreed to the fight unless he thought he was in with a shout at reclaiming the belt. Having to withdraw will also have pissed him off, but that was the situation he found himself in, which, in turn, resulted in me fighting Julius Francis.

To ease Welsh Phil's frustration, he was offered a pop at the winner and, if that was me (for that, now read *is* me), we could hold my first defence in Cardiff or Carlisle. Naturally, as the incumbent Guv'nor, I chose Carlisle. Why the fuck should I have to defend my belt in his home city? If the belt had been around his waist, would he have come to Carlisle for his first defence of the title? I rest my case. Sorry, Phil, but any contest involving the two of us is postponed for the time being at least, perhaps indefinitely – maybe even for good.

But while it was still on the cards, life did get interesting. Yeah, I think that's how I'd describe the antics that went on as Ricky English and Joey Pyle Jnr worked on bringing the two of us together to contest The Guv'nor title.

Let's go back to that first contact when Ricky offered me the chance to realise my dream and become the youngest ever holder of the title, The Guv'nor. It came out of the blue.

Long before he got in touch, I knew who Ricky English was, of course. Everybody in the fight game, including in BKB circles, knows that name. After Frank Warren, he's the busiest fight promoter in the business. Put that name together with Joey Pyle, with whom he was once partnered as a sort of sorcerer's apprentice, and you're entering the realms of fight folklore. Oh yeah, and not long after Joey passed away, Ricky teamed up with the great man's son and heir, Joey Pyle Jnr. Thanks to their love of the sport and commitment, the old legend's legacy continues.

Ricky and Joey Jnr have been friends since they were kids. Ricky, being older, put his arm around little Joey from the tender age of four and soon learned the benefits of hanging with Pyle junior. Ricky tells me that they were a pair of proper scallywags who all too often found themselves in trouble with the Old Bill but Ricky soon learned to let Joey Jnr do the talking if their collars got felt. The minute the cops heard the name Joey Pyle they'd ask after his dad and send them on their way. Such was the respect Joey Pyle enjoyed on their manor. Ricky and Joey Jnr pulled that particular 'get out of the shit' card quite a few times.

Ricky comes from a fighting background himself. His dad,

Billy English, was a very straight man but a real hard bastard. He began his fighting career on the cobbles and in bareknuckle fights before he became a top amateur boxing coach. Growing up in the same neighbourhood, the likes of Joey Pyle looked up to Billy and, when he became 'The Man' on that manor, he took young Ricky under his wing. So as you see, Ricky was raised around fighting and amidst the gangland culture of the late 1960s onwards.

He had 106 fights at light-welter and welterweight in his career before becoming a leading amateur coach in his own right. The guy knows the game from boot straps to bindings; from child protégé to professional promoter. Not only that, Ricky boxed for England and, after living in Canada for a few years, even got on the Canadian National Team but never actually represented the Canucks in competition. Not many fighters are good enough to make one national squad, let alone two. What I'm saying is that he's no fast-talking Flash Harry; Ricky walks the walk and, when he talks fighting, people listen.

As I was saying earlier, one day out of the blue, I received a call from Ricky. Apparently, he'd spotted a link to one of my fights on a friend's Facebook page and, as a result, had been watching some of my fights on YouTube. He started telling me how impressed he had been with what he had seen. I immediately stopped him and told him that, if he wanted to arrange a fight or something, he'd have to talk to my manager.

Ricky said something like, 'Nah, mate. You've got it all wrong. That's not why I'm ringin' yer. I just wanted to tell you that you're good and ask why the fuck you're wastin' yer time and talent bareknuckle fightin', is all.'

That took me by surprise and he was even more impressed

when I told him I'd never been in a boxing gym. So we got talking about the fight game in general, talked about our heroes, and I told him how I'd always dreamed about fighting for The Guv'nor title. His reply to that stunned me. Again, I can't remember the exact words but the craic went something like this:

'Yeah? So why haven't you ever put your name up?'

'I didn't know I could.'

'Yeah, yeah. . . course you can, mate. It's vacant.'

'So you're tellin' me I could fight for The Guv'nor belt?'

'Yeah, that's what I'm sayin', innit?'

'Who do I talk to about that then?'

'Yer talkin' to him, mate. Me! I own the rights to The Guv'nor title. Nobody fuckin' fights for it except through me.'

'You?'

'Yeah. The title, the belt. Mine, mate.'

'So I can just put my name in the hat and the fight's on?'

'More or less. Course, we'd have to dig out another contender but that shouldn't be a problem. It's The Guv'nor belt, for Christ's sake! Plenty o' geezers want a shot at that.'

'I think you'd better talk to Macca.'

And that's exactly what he did. The next thing you know, Ricky and Joey are announcing to the world that Decca Heggie will contest the vacant Guv'nor title against a former holder of the belt, Welsh Phil Davis of London. Positive affirmation in action! I had been telling myself since I was a kid that one day I would show those bullying bastards what I was capable of and become The Guv'nor.

How did Ricky English come to be the owner of The Guv'nor title? Good question. Ricky had caught the unlicensed-boxing bug watching Alan Matlock's semi-pro shows and decided to have a go himself. What better way than to resurrect The Guv'nor belt. So he asked Joey Snr if he could have the belt and title and that old diamond happily passed the mantle to his spiritual son. That was how it all started for him and Ricky has been responsible for staging every Guv'nor bout since the great Lenny McLean retired.

He's overseen the rise and fall of every Guv'nor and wannabe Guv'nor since, from the raw but rock-hard, pub-brawling Steve Aggi, who won it at his first show, to Big Norman Buckland's victory and defences of the title. When Norman retired undefeated, the belt was declared vacant and, all of a sudden, it was 'game on' but, fuck me: little did I know, as I knuckled down to some serious training and dieting in readiness, how often it would almost slip from my grasp! Even experienced hands like Ricky and Joey Jnr were having no end of trouble arranging the event.

Before turning promoter, Ricky ran his own boxing gym in Watford: the biggest in Europe. From that base he turned out some proper tasty fighters. He coached 2012 Olympic super-heavyweight gold-medal winner and pro-heavyweight IBF World Champion Anthony Joshua in his early days. He was even approached to become an Olympic coach but had to turn the job down because he'd just got his professional ticket. These are the kind of credentials Ricky brings to the table when he's negotiating a deal and setting up an event. The geezer – yeah, sorry, but he is – has worked his way up through the game from amateur to pro, from putting on the gloves to putting on a show. He lives and breathes boxing. Do you see why I was so chuffed when he phoned me just to tell me how good he thought I was? This is a guy who really knows the fight game and what he's looking at and what he's looking for in a fighter.

They say nothing worth having ever comes easy. Well, I can vouch for that. The Guv'nor title was my lifelong dream but gaining it put me through the grinder physically and mentally. Much of which was my own doing. For a start, when it comes to training, I'm full on. I push myself really hard and actually enjoy taking myself to the limit. As regards everything else, I'm spontaneous, some might say; a bit of a loose cannon, headstrong for sure, reckless even. Sometimes I do things without thinking them through properly.

I partly blame the state my head's in after all the coke I sniffed and other stuff I took but, then again, I've always been a bugger for making stuff harder than it needs to be, especially for Macca. Quite a few covert and as yet unidentified players did their level best to rob me of my chance, while others poked their nose in where it wasn't wanted or simply got my back up at a time when I didn't need the distraction and even tried to undermine my confidence, whether deliberately or just by failing to recognise the pressure I was feeling. I think those people forgot that to them this was just another boxing match. To me, it was the fight of my life.

Meanwhile, down in the smoke, it seemed that, every time everything looked set, something would happen to fuck it up. The fight was on and off like a pair of hooker's knickers during a busy weekend down the Reeperbahn. For those who don't know, that's the red-light district in Amsterdam – and, *no*, I've never been there but I know a few blokes who have.

For a start, if I remember rightly, the date changed three or four times, and the venue at least four or five. One day it was going to be in Crystal Palace, then Brighton for some reason, then it switched to the Troxy in the East End before heading south of the river again to Crystal Palace – there was even talk of staging it at the MK Dons Stadium.

The pressure had even begun to get to the coolest customer on the team by a long chalk, Macca. I remember at one point him saying, 'I don't care if we have to have on the nearest open space lit by car headlights. You are fighting that Welsh fucker and coming home with that belt.' And he fuckin' meant it – and I would have as well, if push came to shove. Thankfully, it didn't come to that.

Word had got out that Ricky was holding a bareknuckle event. That was a malicious lie. The anonymous sneaky bastards also alleged that Welsh Phil was a 'naughty' doorman with a bad rep. OK, that was possibly true but not the bit about him bringing a small army of naughty doormen from Cardiff to the show to kick-off if he lost. Nor that I would be getting cheered on by an equally rowdy crew from Carlisle who would also be up for a scrap with the Taffs. It was all total bollocks. The show was primarily being staged to raise awareness and funding for a charity Ricky is trying to launch in memory of his little boy, Frankie, who tragically passed away at the age of two and a half years. The charity is known as Frankie's Wish.

Ask yourself: is it likely he'd risk or tolerate Cardiff and Carlisle fight fans getting medieval with each other at an event for which he had such a deeply personal and emotional attachment? No chance! But at every turn, that lie would surface and the venue would withdraw permission.

So, as you can see, Ricky and Joey were having all sorts of ag and headaches just securing a venue, not to mention all the other bollocks like obtaining licenses, organising publicity, pulling in sponsorship and generating ticket sales.

Trust me: getting in the ring and fighting another fella is the easy bit. It's everything else that goes with it that's a fuckin' nightmare. I don't know how long my fighting career will last but one thing's for sure: I won't turn promoter after I hang up my gloves. Punch me in the head if I do. Sorry, that won't work – plenty have tried and I'm still standing. Kick me in the knackers. That should do the trick.

Preparing for a fight, especially one as important as The Guv'nor was to me, takes a great deal of work and total focus. The trouble with me is that I'm easily distracted. Again, I think it's a symptom of the damage I have done to my brain with drink and drugs but, whatever the reason, it doesn't take much to throw me off course. As the fight drew closer, no end of minor irritations – and some pretty heavy situations outside of my control – crept into my daily routine and also got into my head. At times they caused me to react badly, or simply disrupted my ability to channel my energy in a positive way.

One of my biggest problems came from my addiction to Facebook. There's a lot of negativity out there and a lot of shit-stirrers and troublemakers too. As I become better known, I seem to be attract more and more of them. My mistake was to engage with some of these people, who, whether deliberately or through sheer ignorance, occasionally pushed my buttons. What can I say? I have a short fuse at times and, as a result, I was occasionally a little too quick to jump on the computer and knock out a response to something someone had posted about me.

What I should have done from the start, and what I eventually did, was block a lot of people so that I didn't have to see and read what they were writing on my message board.

The worst part of it was that, up until then, I'd been very open and welcoming towards those who wanted to be my 'friend' but I found out the hard way that many of these cyber-friends aren't very friendly. Not only that, I felt I was letting my genuine friends and followers down. The guilt that generated also messed with my head.

Despite all the hassle Ricky and Joey were having and the negativity I kept encountering, I stuck to my training routine as best I could and did my bit to gain publicity for the fight. Hence why I came to be at Crystal Palace that night when Welsh Phil was fighting. I'd gone down to London with Macca to a party at The Blind Beggar, which was also a promotional bash for the fight.

Norman Buckland was there and loads of other faces. Matt Legg, his dad and his old school-mate were also in the crowd and, having become mates at that event in his home town of Milton Keynes, Matt decided to stick with us. Eventually, I went out back to escape the noise so I could record an interview about how I came to be on The Guv'nor ticket. We had it in mind from the outset to go along to Welsh Phil's fight but there was only me, Macca and Steve Anderson and we knew we'd be entering the lion's den down there because it was his home turf. Matt was up for it as well but he had his dad in tow and didn't fancy taking him along in case there was trouble but, bless him, his dad said, 'Just stick me in a taxi, son, and go with your friends.' So he did.

When we got to the venue, at first, the security lads on the door weren't going to let us in but then they clocked Matt was with us and doubts crept in. Word was sent to the management and, all of a sudden, we were made very welcome. Once we were over the doorstep, word quickly spread and Welsh Phil's crew of about twelve to fifteen useful-looking lads started to get a bit agitated and vocal. I'm fairly sure, had we not had Matt with us *and* had Ricky English not stepped up alongside, things might have got proper dodgy.

Matt had also attracted a few other boxers and big lads who were there to watch the fight to our circle and he, of course, he made sure that they all became aware of who I was. Not that Macca and I were all that bothered. In fact, I think he was a lot cooler than I was about the situation. He was buzzing actually. You have to remember that Macca was ex-BCF, so facing off to a bunch of snarling cockneys took him back to the good old, bad old days when his firm would find themselves confronted by Millwall's F-Troop or West Ham's Inter-City Firm or the Chelsea Headhunters, to name but three rival London outfits.

All I was worried about was that, if it did kick off, I might damage my hands knocking out some of those gobby arseholes and that, as a result, the fight would be postponed. By the time Phil spotted me and started his raving-maniac routine in the ring, we had quite a tasty-looking firm of our own to match his hostile posse. Watch the video clip on YouTube – it's fuckin' hysterical. Phil went absolutely ape-shit, screaming at me, calling me a mug and a northern c**t – but, of course, like all Londoners, he pronounces it 'cant', which somehow doesn't sound quite as offensive to us northern c**ts! Look 'cant' up in the Oxford English Dictionary. Now look up 'c**t'. I can wait. . . See what I mean?

In response to all his threats and insults, I simply smiled and threw a few shadow-boxing moves, which probably made him worse, but nobody can deny that it was a spectacular face-off – far more animated than the nose-to-nose bullshit or standing with fists raised at each other for the photo-opportunity. On the QT, I think Ricky and Jamie thought it was brilliant and, after we left the venue, we had a right laugh about it.

I said something like, 'Fuckin' hell. I thought Welsh Phil's crew was proper gonna kick-off there for a minute.'

Macca, with a grin as broad as a croc that's spotted a big, fat, juicy pig floating past on a lilo, turned to me and said, 'Nah, an' if they had, Matt would have cleaned up half of 'em, you the rest and I could have picked off the stragglers.'

Ever the general, Macca had weighed up the opposition, decided on a strategy and how he'd deploy his troops and win the battle. That's why he's such a good manager: he's always two steps ahead of everyone else and, unlike my other managers, knew he was backing a winner.

CHAPTER SIXTEEN

FERTILE GROUND
FOR A FIGHTER

I'm not offering it as an excuse for the way I turned out but Carlisle does have a violent and lawless history. For the best part of three hundred years it was at the epicentre of an ungovernable territory known as The Debateable Lands. The whole frontier from the Solway Firth into the Lothians of southern Scotland and north Northumberland was riven with bands of roving rustlers, robbers, murderers and mercenaries, known back then as Moss Troopers.

If, like Macca, you're into history, you should read up on that period in this part of the country. There are loads of books about the Reivers or you can Google it and read up about them on Wikipedia. What amazes me is that nobody has ever made a good TV series or major film about them. These were dangerous times on a disputed frontier ruled by the Reivers, who were proper bad bastards. So bad that they invented the crime of blackmail and the word 'bereave' entered our language, from being killed by Reivers – 'to be reived' became 'bereaved'. The OED definition states 'deprive of a relation, friend, etc. especially by death.' You see? I do not make this shit up.

Surnames such as Armstrong, Graham, Elliot, Hetherington, Kerr, Carleton, Scott, Johnstone and Maxwell are still commonplace around Carlisle and the wider area. Those were some of the larger, more powerful clans of the seventy-six Reiver clans that ran amok around here for three centuries or more. I'm no history scholar and, to tell you the truth, I'm a long way from being an expert on the Reivers but I'm convinced their instincts for survival and their readiness for a scrap are in the DNA of all us borderers.

Because of its turbulent history, Carlisle has always been a hard place and, being the region's only city, it attracts folk from far and wide. People from towns and villages all over the border area head this way, either to shop or for a good night out. Naturally, when gangs of lads from different places converge in the city centre, at weekends in particular, it can get very lively, especially when you add alcohol to the mix. Despite all you hear on the news about drunken violence in and around our towns and cities these days, it's nothing new. Carlisle's Botchergate has been synonymous with heavy drinking and rowdiness for more than two hundred years.

By virtue of its location, the Scots often came marauding into what is now the city since the days of the Picts (they still do) and would do a little more pillaging as they legged it back across the border. Nowadays, though, it's by the bus or train-load and, from time to time, those ancient Jock and Sassenach rivalries come to the surface. But it's the local incomers you are most likely to find roaming the city and acting a bit frisky.

If it's not incomers, lads from Carlisle can just as easily find cause for a fight with each other. Been there, done that, had the T-shirt torn off my back. Only to be expected when you're from Old Harraby – we just call it growing pains.

In the media we hear a lot about London's postcode gang culture. However, before postcodes came into being, rivalry between different boroughs was just as rife. It was no different in Carlisle. The Wrecking Crew, for instance, who later became known as The Chest Waders, for reasons best known to themselves, were mostly made up of mods and scooter boys. To the south of the city, Raffles Midnight Runners were a particularly tasty mob.

Wherever you went in Carlisle back then, there was a gang that identified with that area: the Melbourne Casuals, the Denton Republican Army, the East End Boot Boys, the West End Boot Boys, the Upperby Mad Mob and Morton Skins, born of the skinhead fad that began in the late 1960s. Finally, my home turf's Harraby Skins, who favoured donkey jackets or those military-green bomber jackets and combat fatigues tucked into high-leg boots, a look that became associated with far-right skinhead gangs. I'm not sure whether the New and Old Harraby lads had any particular political leanings but I doubt they were Lib-Dems.

For years these gangs remained rivals, entrenched on their estates in Carlisle but regularly running sorties onto rival turf for a bit of excitement that inevitably led to a tear-up. With so many of these rival factions being supporters of Carlisle United, though, they were slowly, and sometimes reluctantly, drawn together to form the Border City Firm: Carlisle United's passionate but ultra-violent supporters.

I'm told that, for a while, you could still tell some of the crews apart because of the way they dressed. The casuals among them, known as *dressers*, became the main influence on the style of the BCF, which eventually resulted in a smart crew of top boys who made their mark on the football-hooligan scene. After winning respect from other outfits up and down the country, hardcore members of the BCF were soon to be found at the heart of the notorious England Casuals. They followed our national team and caused bother wherever they went, all over Europe.

Long before any of these lads started flexing their muscles and getting into turf wars, there were the biker gangs. Angus Dalton, God rest his soul, passed away in August 2016. In 1976 he founded the Rogue Angels Motor Cycle Club and, shortly afterwards, formed a close bond with Glasgow's infamous Blue Angels, the oldest biker gang in Europe. Angus and his outfit weren't just motor-cycle enthusiasts that got dressed up as a biker gang. This was a lifestyle choice and they were the real deal. Theirs was a fraternity that lived according to its own set of rules and outside the laws of the land. To be 'patched' was to make a lifelong commitment to the gang; to become a sworn member of a brotherhood. Nobody took it more seriously than Angus Dalton Snr and he was known and respected by other biker-gang members as far afield as Holland.

By 1989 the Rogue Angels had morphed into the Cycle Gypsies, who, in turn, became affiliated to the Devil's Disciples and, eventually, were 'patched over' by the Disciples to become their Carlisle Chapter. Before they amalgamated with the Disciples, mind, and while still bearing the colours of the Cycle Gypsies, they went to war with the BCF. And I mean war! It got proper ugly and extremely dangerous for any member of those two rival gangs on the streets of the city for quite a while. Unfortunately for the BCF, it was a case of men versus boys.

The rivalry erupted after Macca had walked away from the BCF but that didn't stop several of the bikers paying him a visit. It was a touchy moment from which he emerged unscathed, partly out of respect but mainly because they realised there was little love lost by then between him and the notorious hooligan gang he'd help found. In fact, Macca was betrayed by the very BCF ring leader at the top of their hit-list. Consequently, he had little sympathy for his former BCF ally – a lad whose evidence had seen him charged with a serious assault he didn't commit, remanded in prison in the Isle of Man and, as a result, put on trial.

Justice was eventually served, though: Macca was found not guilty. And the lad who lied about him to the police? The Cycle Gypsies eventually caught up with him and, in broad daylight, on Warwick Road, Carlisle, reduced his BMW to scrap metal as he sat cowering inside.

My dad's told me tales of the 1970s and a local 'face' known as Vic 'The Brick' Kelleher. Macca, too, having been in the BCF, knows a few craics about Vic The Brick as well. It was Vic that put together a small but useful firm of like-minded troublemakers from all over the city and began hiring buses to attend Carlisle away games. They'd rendezvous at the Dive Bar and plan the day's mayhem from there. Vic is credited among the hooligan fraternity with being one of the first to export border-city football violence to rival grounds all over Britain.

Vic once told Macca about the first time he made the booking through Blair and Palmers, a local coach-hire firm.

The bloke who was in charge that day was expecting a coach-load of Carlisle United supporters. What he got was a mob of around fifty rough-looking young men in boots and braces. Vic said the poor bugger's face turned ashen and he thought the fella was going to have a heart attack.

The 1960s had seen the rise of the mods-and-rockers wars at resorts all over Britain and, by the late 1960s, that brand of mob violence had spread to the football terraces. I don't know if Vic the Brick's outfit was the first at Carlisle United but soon others began to emerge. Naughty outfits, such as the Motley Crew (not to be confused with the famous rock band of the same name) used to meet upstairs in The Cumberland Arms on match days. From their first-floor vantage point, they'd watch out for potential targets passing or entering the pub beneath them or other boozers down Botchergate, then spring their ambush.

Go back to the 1960s and names like John Stubbs from Raffles – a local singer and ex-rugby-league player in the local amateur league – crop up. He put together 'The Sheenies' – the name comes from those living on Sheenhan Crescent on the Raffles estate. Big John and his brother Fred teamed up with Crocket and Kenny Ewing and their kid brother. Kenny was Macca's neighbour when he was a kid. Most people will remember Big John Stubbs as a singer on the pubs-and-clubs circuit of the county. He was reputed to have a terrific voice but he was just as capable of tuning you up with his fists. He moved away from Carlisle to somewhere down south.

His old mate Kenny turned into a bit of a career criminal, eventually running the heroin trade in Carlisle. Even though he was one of the drugs kingpins of the city's underworld, Macca tells me he used to knock on their door and ask his mum what shift Macca's dad, Matt, was on. That was so he knew whether he could play his music without annoying him. Yeah, as you might have guessed, Macca's dad was no slouch back in the day. Kenny died of an overdose.

After the Sheenies days, two more rival gangs ran amok around the Raffles estate and regularly got into gear with each other. The Shady Boys off Shady Grove Road and The Bowers, or Bower Boys, from Bower Street. At some point they made peace and came to together to form Raffles Midnight Runners. That tasty crew never took a backward step against any rival gang. Lads like Sweet, Cherry, Raymond the Rock Box, Boogie Brian and many more form part of Raffles folklore now. Macca tells me that they saved the skins of the BCF one fateful day at a home game against Blackburn Rovers.

Macca's firm, the BCF, were on the way to the match when they found themselves well outnumbered by Blackburn's notorious, but unimaginatively named, Blackburn Youth. Macca tells me that, earlier that day, he had arranged to meet Raffles finest in the back room of the Cally (The Caledonian on Botchergate). He worked with Raymond the Rock Box and had arranged to meet him for a few beers before join the rest of the firm for the trip down to Brunton Park, or 'Fortress Brunton', as it was known to them. Macca recalled a lad from Brampton being with them who was a sort of affiliated member of their crew. Macca and a few of the lads said their goodbyes to the Raffles elite and made their way to the ground. By the time they reached Warwick Road to join other members of the BCF, they found themselves overwhelmed by sheer weight of numbers. Blackburn Youth had turned up intent on a huge show of force. Some BCF lads lost their bottles, back-peddling (running, in football terms) in the face of the enemy, which lads like Macca considered a disgrace, especially on their home turf. Blackburn Youth had begun to gain the upperhand as the more ballsy BCF casuals fought running battles with them in the network of streets near to Brunton Park, Carlisle United's ground.

Blackburn Youth looked set to take the honours until, all of a sudden, a white transit van screeched to a halt beside them. Dressed in their trademark donkey jackets or sheepskin car-coats and wearing Doc Martens or more heavy-duty, military-grade, high-leg boots, about ten of the Raffles Midnight Runners jumped out of the back. Outnumbered by dozens, they faced off and, for a minute, Blackburn Youth hadn't a clue what to do. Macca and his boys did, though: back-up the Midnight Runners and fuckin' do the bastards.

Those ten guys led the charge and tore into them like Tasmanian devils. Sweet was definitely among them, as was The Rock Box, Cherry and Boogie Brian. My apologies to those whose names are missing but your timely intervention has gone down in Carlisle football-hooligan legend. Those lads turned the tide of the battle, forcing Blackburn Youth into retreat. Carlisle pride was restored. About twenty minutes into the game, the Raffles lads appeared selling trendy leather jackets and other clothes they had taken from the backs of the fallen Blackburn firm. Then they began their familiar terrace chant:

'R-A-F-F-L-E-S – Raffles Boot Boys are the best.'

And after helping them see off a much bigger firm, Macca said they undoubtedly were! It was also a memorable day for the worst possible reasons. It was one of those days when the police were either undermanned or overstretched but they'd struggled to keep the warring factions apart before the game and afterwards. Organised from inside the paddock, a heavy number of true fighting men formed the intent of settling things with the Blackburn hooligans who goaded them from above on the terraces. Despite being shepherded out of the ground, the cops were soon running around like headless chickens as violence broke out all over the place between the ground, the city and the railway station.

It was a strategy that had worked before. Younger and less effective members of the BCF would disperse in different directions to hunt down away supporters and draw the cops after them. Meanwhile, the hardcore would concentrate on their equals in the away faction. That is what happened and it was carnage. The BCF and Raffles Midnight Runners were confident, still revelling in their earlier rout of Rovers' visiting hooligans as they clashed with them again.

Many lads from both sides were hurt badly but the adrenaline was pumping and the thirst for blood was being quenched. Macca told me exactly where he was when he noticed a guy going down near a telegraph pole. It looked, to him, like the boy had been hit by someone holding a cobble or half-brick. But there was so much going on that it was hard to tell who was doing what to who? Eventually, the Old Bill arrived in greater numbers and broke it up but not before they, too, were almost overwhelmed by the sheer level of violence.

As the rival fans were parted, one guy was still lying there covered in blood and motionless beside a telegraph pole. The cops caused the crowds to disperse but there were mutterings.

'He's dead.'

Those words spread like Chinese whispers, even as the rival hooligans met up again and again to fight on in small pockets all the way up Warwick Road and beyond. That night battle scars were proudly shown and stories of glorious victories were exchanged as the beer flowed. Eventually, the drunken youth of Carlisle made their way home and Macca remembers his dad shouting up the stairs to him, 'Hey, boy! Get your arse down here. You've got visitors.'

Once roused from his pit, he was met downstairs by four dour-looking, plain-clothes coppers, who questioned him for a while and pulled no punches about how serious the situation was. The lad who he'd been having a pre-match pint with in the Cally had breathed his last that day. Out of respect for his family, I won't name him. It was a very dark day in the history of Carlisle United. Thankfully, that blight on the beautiful game seems to have run its course, at least at a domestic level.

I included these stories in mine so as to illustrate that, even in my small but ancient city, violence is never far from the surface. Fighting and gang rivalry has always been an integral part of border-city life, from the time of the Picts to the lawless Reivers; from the Biker gangs to the hooligans of the BCF. It might not hit the headlines like it used to but it still goes on. It's in our nature – innit!

Down the years, the city's turbulent history has spawned some very hard men indeed. I'm talking about men so tough you would think they'd been born in the red-hot heat of a blacksmith's forge and beaten into shape on an anvil. But Carlisle wasn't the only place that bred hard-men in our county.

Too many for me to list or do justice to in this book earned their hard reputations around Carlisle the only way men like them can: by taking on and beating anyone who challenged them; hard-men who never took a step back and, often as not, emerged the victor, no matter what the odds. Not all of them were nice men, yet some of them were proper gents, respected for their principles as much as their physical presence, fighting ability and meet-it-head-on approach to life in general and trouble, whenever it reared its head. What they all had in common was grit and courage, fighting prowess and uncompromising mettle that set them apart from the average brawler and handy lad.

Mention Cumbria and most people think of the Lake District – rightly so: it's truly a beautiful place; a jewel in Britain's varied landscape. What people might not associate with my home county is coal mining, steel production and heavy industry. Carlisle remains a centre for heavy engineering, despite the national downturn since the late 1970s. Not only that but it's very much an agricultural county and farming breeds its fair share of big, strong, strapping lads who aren't shy of stepping outside for a straightener when challenged.

Travel down west towards the steel town of Workington and on to Whitehaven and you'll pass through age-old mining communities and former fishing ports, which line the coast from Port Carlisle to Barrow. Another centre of shipbuilding and heavy industry until the boundary changes in 1973 was in Lancashire. Then there is the county's main industry: farming and agriculture.

Why am I telling you this? Well, it harks back to certain attitudes I have mentioned in this book, which I have witnessed first-hand: that we Cumbrians are all sheep-shagging, country bumpkins! The reality is that communities such as those I have mentioned have traditionally spawned hard-men. Carlisle and Cumberland, as it was once known, have produced some really tough blokes that, to this day, I would back against many another hard-man from anywhere around the UK.

While I'm in the 'respect' zone, I'd like to take this

opportunity to make a special mention of a dear friend for whom I have immense respect, Ryan Kinely.

Ryan is not a fighter or a tough-guy or hard-man but I admire him as much, if not more than any of the men I have mentioned in this book. Ryan is one of the most loving and caring men I have ever met. He has Down syndrome and holds a special place in my heart.

Ryan lives each day with such optimism, joy, determination and courage and he never complains about the restrictions his condition places on him. It could be argued that, having been born with the condition, he knows no difference but Ryan is very aware that he is different from us. Like many people who live with a disability, he has a much deeper understanding of his situation than we sometimes give such people credit for.

The story of how I met Ryan goes like this: I got chatting with a really beautiful girl called Taylor Rae Hamilton via social media. It turned out that she lived in Northern Ireland. Taylor is a model and the winner of beauty pageant competitions and, as it turned out, a bit of a celeb over there. I didn't have to think twice when I received an invitation to visit and, from the moment I got there, we began dating. I couldn't believe I was going out with a girl as stunning as Taylor.

Naturally, her family wanted to meet this bareknuckle fighter she'd invited over from Carlisle. They couldn't have been more welcoming and the loveliest of them all was her uncle, Ryan. Ryan's equally lovely mum, Ann, invited me to stay with them on my visits and the whole family have become very close friends.

Taylor and her uncle are very close and that was another thing I found very attractive about her. She doted on Uncle Ryan and obviously loves him to bits, as he does her. Although it didn't work out for us (the distance between Carlisle and Belfast was the biggest problem), we remain friends and I've kept in contact with all of them.

If I'm being honest, the travelling wasn't the only problem. I was crazy about her and used to get quite jealous of all the attention she attracted. It was inevitable: she's drop-dead gorgeous. As I said before, she's fairly well known, particularly around Belfast, and has appeared on TV a few times. As a result, we couldn't go anywhere without her attracting attention, especially from blokes. I could have got myself into some real serious bother over Taylor and almost did more than once.

The Kinelys and Hamiltons all follow my career and I regularly talk to Ryan and his mum on the phone. I spent a memorable Christmas with the Hamilton family in 2014. By then, Ryan and I had formed a strong bond. They refer to people like Ryan as having 'special needs'. I'm not sure he needs anything more than he has: the love and devotion of his very close family. Ryan is definitely special – he's a beautiful person. This warm, loving man taught me to appreciate life more and respect people more.

During that brief stay, on Boxing Day, I was alone with him and chatting about this and that and somehow he reached into me and saw through the front I put on as a rough, tough, fighting Jack-the-lad. I broke down and began to cry but it felt OK to do that with him. I knew Ryan wouldn't judge me or think of me as weak. To comfort me, that sweet man said something I'll never forget: 'Decca, I love you and I will never let anyone hurt you.'

He meant it. To Ryan, my size and strength and the things I have done aren't what define me; it's what inside that matters and that is all that mattered to him. I'll never forget what he said and that's why I will always feel a bond of love for my friend Ryan. My biggest regret about the night of the Guv'nor title fight was that Ryan could not be there in London when I won. I so wanted him to lead me out into that arena and be at my table afterwards to join in the celebrations but I know he was there in spirit and willing me on all the way.

Special needs? *Nah!* Special person. More impressive and courageous than any of the men I have previously mentioned, including me, and my story would not be complete without this tribute to him. I love you, Ryan. You're the best and bravest of us all.

CHAPTER SEVENTEEN

THE GUV'NOR

Finally, we have arrived at the end of a very, very long road; one that began as a bullied boy's seemingly impossible dream. Except I never stopped dreaming or believing! That is the secret to achieving your dreams. It only ever becomes a reality if you refuse to give up and never lose sight of the prize. Don't make the mistake of thinking it will come easy, though. Anything worth having rarely does. Be prepared to have your faith and self-belief, your principles and patience, your mind and body tested and tested again. It is only by pushing on through that process that you'll emerge a winner.

Are you a believer in astrology? I am. Oh, I can hear some of you groan from here and I know that scientists like Professor Brian Cox roll their eyes at its mention. As it happens, I'm a great admirer of his, so bear me out. Like I said earlier, I'm into all that stuff about our solar system and the universe and always tune into Professor Cox's programmes.

The thing is that I once saw him on *Stargazing Live* talking about sub-atomic particles and what they're made up of and he said that every little physical thing we do ripples through the entire cosmos. From opening our eyes to detonating an atomic bomb, everything has an effect on the space around us. Imagine that! It's something to do with some sub-atomic particles being unable to share the same space. Don't ask me which sub-atomic particles but that's what Professor Cox said and he's a fella that seems to know his stuff.

I don't claim to understand all the complex physics that he used to explain why it happens but, in my head, it boiled down to cause and effect; action and reaction. Everything we do makes those particles move and the ones next to them move and so it goes on, right through the universe, each particle bumping into the next and having to make room for its neighbour, causing a ripple effect. Fair enough: that makes sense. Let's face it, these top physicists are all very clever fuckers and have worked all this shit out, so I'm convinced – but wait!

How can the professor then deny that the movement of the planets is going to have an effect on us? According to him, it must. If the blink of an eye can send ripples through the universe, surely the rotation of the planets and the orbits of their moons around them, and then the whole fuckin' lot around the sun, must create a greater ripple effect than me winking at a mate?

Astrology might not be everybody's cup of tea but, as a science, it's a much older one than astronomy. If you don't believe me, check out the charts they use and all the complex calculations it takes to make the predictions they make. I don't doubt some of the people that claim to use astrology are con-artists but it's an ancient practice and there are just as many practitioners who take it very seriously indeed.

But what do I know? I'm just a guy who punches other guys and gets punched for a living. OK, well I know this: my stars predicted a turbulent time in the build-up to my fight for the Guv'nor title and that, because of a powerful full moon on the day and night of the fight, nothing would go quite as expected – and boy, were they ever right. What a strange weekend it turned into.

Shortly before 11am on Saturday, 15 October 2016, we gathered at Carlisle railway station. There was me, Macca, Carl Lewthwaite, Stephen Wood and a last minute, but no less welcome member of the team, Ian 'Chem' Chambers, who, unlike the rest of us, didn't have a first-class ticket. No big deal – he'd upgrade on the train, he said. What mattered to me was that he'd made the effort. He was there, supporting his mate and determined to see him fight for The Guv'nor title and I was chuffed to bits, as were the others. Not only that, he's as funny as fuck.

Almost right away our travel plans got disrupted. Macca, as ever, was double-checking every detail. Good job too. He noticed that our train was running on time but that we were on the wrong platform. Our train was coming in on platform three. Platform three? That didn't make sense. Platform three is usually designated to trains heading north to Glasgow and Edinburgh. We were going in the opposite direction. The lads queried it and went to look for themselves but, sure enough, according to the electronic timetable and the Virgin staff busily shepherding passengers about, our train was arriving at platform three.

Still puzzled, we humped all our gear over the bridge, as

directed, and waited. As the train rolled into Carlisle, the announcement came over the loudspeaker of its imminent arrival on... platform one – the very platform we'd been happily waiting on before getting directed across the tracks! *Shit!* We were on the wrong side of the station. There was a bit of swearing and grumbling – a lot actually – and a right old, every-man-for-himself, passenger stampede back over the bridge, followed by a proper scrum once those doors opened. Not that anyone troubled us: a former heavyweight bare-knuckle fighting champion and unlicensed boxer, two ex-amateur rugby-league players, a former champion bodybuilder and an ex-copper. No amount of barging was going to stop us getting on as we calmly claimed our places in the first-class carriage. Not a great start but, finally, we were underway.

Just the day before, Chem had been doing a leg workout at his gym with a competitive bodybuilder called David Hannah, who is in incredible shape for a guy of fifty-seven. Every session under Chem's instruction is a proper beasting but legs are a bit of a speciality and he doesn't spare himself when doing the routine with you. Been there, done that – and could barely walk afterwards. Chem said that Dave can match him weight for weight but not when it comes to the number of reps he can knock out. As a result, he was still absolutely knackered when he got onto the train and promptly fell asleep.

As per instructions, I'd been drinking water by the litre and soon needed to go to the loo, which just happened to coincide with the guard coming along to check our tickets. Carl handed them over: four first-class tickets, four bodies in seats, one of whom was fast asleep. I swear that it was a pure coincidence that I was on the bog. Cheers, gents: job done. He moved on and Chem slept first-class the whole way with his standard ticket in his arse pocket. Ah, well, train tickets are a rip-off anyway and, although only a small victory, no less sweet. Macca had tried to cancel and switch our return tickets after all the venue and dates changes but Virgin wouldn't let him. Money-grubbing twats!

After a while, Carl went for a wander down the train and returned to tell us he'd spotted Paddy Doherty a few carriages back. What were the odds that there would be two former bareknuckle fighters riding the same train? Paddy's a legend on the gypsy BKF circuit. If you tuned in to the show, you'll have seen him in *My Big Fat Gypsy Wedding* or as the overall winner of *Celebrity Big Brother* but he's much better known, in my circles, as a proper tasty fighter and, like so many hardmen, he's a really nice fella and a gentleman.

Anyway, we decided to walk down the train for a chat and take advantage of a photo opportunity with a fellow fighter I truly admire. Paddy couldn't have been more welcoming and pleased that we took the trouble. He was heading for London on family business and wouldn't be able to attend the fight but wished me all the luck in the world. The luck of the Irish then, because I won. However, I'm getting ahead of myself. We talked about some of the people we both know and how it is, as a fighter, just trying to keep out of trouble.

Paddy told us a great craic about a big fella that landed in his local to take him on. This great big, stupid sausage of a rugby type, as Paddy described him, had got it into his head that he couldn't lose if he fought Paddy. He'd either take a famous bareknuckle fighter's scalp or have a story to sell to the *Sun*. Listen, fellas, Paddy may be fifty-seven but believe me: his fists still think they're in their prime. Anyway, to cut a long story short, within minutes of Paddy arriving the sausage made his play and provoked the fight he had turned up looking for and ended up star-fished for his trouble.

Out of the blue, the boys in blue turned up. The question is: who the hell called them? The sneaky sausage must have had someone primed to call 999 to save his cowardly arse if it went pear-shaped because nobody in the pub phoned them. The cops landed and questions were asked and the idiot nicked for a breach of the peace.

Do you remember when I explained that the guy with the injuries isn't necessarily the victim – just the loser? Well, there you have a classic example. All Paddy had gone to his local for was a pint with his mates. He was already on a fizzer and looking at jail time if he slipped up, so that sort of trouble was the last thing he was looking for, or needed. Had there been no witnesses he'd have been up shit creek.

We arrived on schedule in the smoke and, after a short journey via the underground and the DLR, got to the hotel to find another friend and sponsor (from Manhattan, New York), Josephine Ambrosino, waiting there for us. Even though I knew she was coming, when Josephine appeared at the door to my room, I was still blown away. Having sent me money every month to help get me achieve my dream, this amazing lady had gone to the additional trouble and expense of travelling all the way from New York to see me engage in the biggest fight of my life.

Josephine's support and friendship has been unwavering and I was overjoyed to finally meet her. In no time at all, it was as if we'd known each other for years. It's those meaningful and sincere deeds such as Josephine's that make me feel humble and privileged to be where I am today. Only one man can wear The Guv'nor belt but it takes the commitment of many to get that man to that arena. My heartfelt thanks go out to all of them. You know who you are.

After freshening up, we hit the streets of London's East End and eventually arrived at The Blind Beggar, which, thanks to the mad and murderous Ronnie Kray, is quite possibly London's most infamous public house. Naturally, with the biggest fight in my life but a day away, I wasn't interested in a session on the ale and, in any case, I don't really drink at all these days. I went with Chem and Josephine for a meal in a nearby Thai restaurant and left the others in the pub. Surprisingly, nobody ended up getting hammered but one or two of our party had a little more of a roll in their gait as we headed back to the hotel. For me, it was a case of straight to bed but the others headed for the hotel bar and enjoyed a nightcap – or should I say several nightcaps? – before retiring.

The following morning I bounced down for breakfast bright and breezy, as did Chem and Stephen, who beat us all to the spread and looked pretty limber too. The others... well, they were a little bit worse for wear but, being old hands, weren't going to let a bit of a hangover get the better of them. Poor Josephine had discovered why we Brits scoff about American beers being as weak as 'pish'. She'd tried a couple of pints – maybe three – and then supped too many glasses of red wine when we got back to the hotel. To be fair, despite being a little bleary-eyed, she coped pretty well: they breed these Italian-Americans tough. Ask John Gotti if you don't believe me. Oh, and did I mention that she sported a known mafia tag in the form of a tattoo on one of her fingers and the word 'Omerta' (the word for the code of silence practised by the Mafia) on her forearm?

My plan for the big day was to eat regularly, drink plenty

of water, relax and do nothing more energetic than walk around the hotel and local neighbourhood. Josephine elected to stay with me, and the others, guided by Carl, headed for Camden Market.

They hadn't been gone all that long when Steve Anderson arrived from Northampton to join the team. He, too, decided to hang out with me. We spent the day talking about the rocky road that had led me to this title fight and my strategy for defeating my enormous opponent. Steve, like me, has been a lifelong fan of Lenny McLean and some of the other Guv'nors that followed. He's watched every fight, from those grainy recordings of Lenny taking on the likes of Mad Gypsy Bradshaw and Roy Shaw to Norman Buckland's reign. He also used to do a bit of MMA fighting, so he knows the score.

I explained that I'd been working mainly on my stamina and power during boxing sessions. Taking on an experienced man-mountain like Julius wasn't going to be easy, so I'd focused on getting as fit as possible, knowing it was very likely to go the distance. As for my game-plan, once the bell sounded, combinations of body-shots to blow the wind out of Julius, followed by upper-cuts and methods of getting past his defence to target his chin.

Steve thought my strategy pretty sound. Going for a knockout was not out of the question. I can bang pretty good but, that said, knocking Julius out would have been a real challenge for anyone. Ask the likes of Mike Tyson, Vitali Klitchko or Danny Williams, to name but three. Guys like him don't go down easy and I'd pretty much decided that it would probably take every second of every round to secure a win. As a consequence, I had prepared to go the distance. The question was: could I overcome his size and experience, and get past his defence to land a knockout shot? Only a few hours remained before I would know the answer to that question and the butterflies had already started.

Don't misunderstand that last line about butterflies. I don't get overly nervous prior to a fight but I am only human. I know I'm going to get hurt, especially against a giant like Julius, who can land shots like rocks to the head. So anybody who says they don't care about being hit that hard or who doesn't fear pain is either insane or a liar. Yes, I did say at the start of the book that I like getting hit. The effect fuels my adrenaline and makes me fight all the harder but it still fuckin' hurts. I always have that fear in my gut that this just might be the guy with the skills and power to defeat me.

Meanwhile, somewhere up the M6, my dad was on his way with my clothes for the after-fight party. There is always a party to attend after a big fight and, win or lose, I was expected to be there. Dad was travelling down in his mate Kenny's car with another friend of mine, Robbo, from Workington. Just north of Rugby they were involved in a four-car pile-up that wrecked the front end of Kenny's motor and caused minor injuries to both Dad and Robbo.

You can imagine the effect that news had on me as the pre-fight tension built. Fortunately, my cousin Johnny and a couple of mates were also southbound to see the fight so they threw a U-turn and scooped Dad and Robbo up, along with my spare clothing. In pain but determined to be there, the two old warriors pressed on to London. Sadly, Kenny was detained for questioning and had to organise the recovery of his motor. Do you see where I'm going with this? The stars predicted that nothing would go to plan and, once again, they had been proved right.

All too soon, the time was upon us. We got into two matching black Mercedes private-hire cars and were driven in convoy through the city's nightscape to the Clapham Grand, south of the River Thames. Along the way we took in quite a few of the sights – St Paul's, the Tower of London, Tower Bridge and the Houses of Parliament – as we crawled through heavy traffic from the East End along the Thames Embankment towards Clapham and destiny.

We were greeted upon arrival by Julius's larger-than-life manager, Teddy Bam-Bam, who was also running the event's security. Teddy isn't very tall but his gigantic personality makes him stand out in any crowd and it can be a little overwhelming. After a few hugs and handshakes, we were ushered in past the doormen and a rapidly growing queue and into the foyer, where I was immediately collared by a camera crew and had a mic shoved in my face. I'd have preferred to go straight to my dressing room but these are the things you have to do when you're fighting for The Guv'nor title.

I played my part and gave them the spiel I'd rehearsed in my head, all of which was true and heartfelt, if a little repetitive. I've learned never to go off script because any variation on what you have previously said can be misinterpreted. Interview over, we were whisked through the venue and through a warren of corridors and stairwells to the room where I would get my gear on and go through my ritual preparations.

Macca elected to stay with me to monitor the comings and goings of those who wanted to wish me well or just say hi. Also in the room virtually the whole of the time were Matt Legg, my corner man for the night, Steve Anderson and Stephen Wood, who was taking notes and names. I don't mind telling you that I have never been as tense before a fight as I was that night. It was great to see and receive so many well-wishers but it doesn't help when you're trying to focus your mind and channel your energy. Below, in the ring, Ricky was introducing the real heroes of the night: the first two fighters, Colin Wood's adaptive boxers, Luke 'Lukey Boy' Milligan and Brian Lever, who, by all accounts, stunned the watching audience with their courage, mobility, agility and skills.

Discussions are already underway with both England Boxing, AIBA (The World governing body for amateur boxing) and the Olympic Committee for adaptive boxing to become eligible as a Paralympic sport in the near future. The ABO support amputee (leg and arm) boxers and are willing to consider licensing amputees should they meet the stringent medical standards required.

I wish I could have been ringside watching and cheering them on as Lukey Boy took the honours but my place was with Matt Legg getting psyched and ready. By then, I'd also been joined by one of Matt's protégés, Ashley Jones, another heavyweight who was on the bill. It helped having Ashley there and watching him prepare. That boy packs a punch. I was proper impressed with his work on the pads and the speed and power he got into his combinations.

As the minutes ticked by, though, I slowly disconnected from what was going on around me and went into myself. It's a zone I cannot share with anyone else and one that is almost impossible to describe. I hear hundreds of voices in my head – voices from the past, like the bullies, the critics and the doubters, but there are others who encourage me as well. I can't always make sense of them but I listen intently. The trouble is that well-meaning visitors silence them. When they're gone and the door closes, the voices return. Then I picture my opponent; the man that stands between me and victory. I visualise how I will overcome him as I prepare myself mentally for the punishment I'm about take. Once I'm through the ropes, I'll be all right. The moment we tap gloves, I'll give all; every ounce of my energy, even to death. I'll be unstoppable.

Below, in the auditorium, just as the stars had predicted, little was going to plan. There was confusion over tables and seating arrangements. Teddy was apparently letting people in who weren't on the guest list and didn't have tickets and, worst of all, two scheduled fighters failed to turn up. All this chaos below kept filtering back to my room but, to be honest, I didn't want to know. What fighter wants to hear that everything's going to rat-shit when they're preparing for the biggest fight of their life?

Then Ashley went down to face his opponent. I wished him well and, as I waited for Matt to return, I did some stretching, press-ups and shadow-boxing. Then, once again, those star predictions proved ominous. Ashley's fight was over in the first few seconds but not by a knockout. A simple clash of heads while Ashley was on the ropes saw his opponent retaliate with a deft head-butt to Ashley's left eye-socket that split the skin of his cheek. As Ashley went down, grappling with the lad, the ref bailed in, the corner men pounced on the melee and all sorts of folk were clambering into the ring. Ricky was on the mic screaming for order. After a face-off between the two corners, the ring was eventually cleared and the two boxers were brought to the middle to tap gloves and part with the promise of a rematch. Sorted, but not in the way fighters ever wish to see a contest end.

Ashley landed back in our room with a nasty cut and a

shiner developing and Matt, still furious, quickly followed. No time to brood over that shambles. We had to prepare. Ashley did a quick change and left the room to take his seat for my fight. No sooner had Ashley gone than Dean Warwick appeared to bind my hands. Dean's a wiry ex-lightweight who still lives and breathes boxing. He took a great deal of care and time making sure my bindings were just as I wanted them and kept stopping to let me flex my fingers. I nodded. 'Perfect. Crack on, Dean,' I said, offering my other hand.

Hands bound I, slipped into my 10oz gloves and Matt got the pads on to begin my warm-up routine. Now I was totally focused, slamming the pads and listening to his advice as we circled each other in that confined claustrophobic space.

'Remember,' Matt said, staring into my eyes. 'You can't make every shot count but it only takes one, so pour it on and keep moving. Julius will let you come on to him and will pick his shots. So hit and move.' And that is what we rehearsed. My confidence was growing with every heavy slap of the glove into those pads, accompanied by Matt's encouraging words of approval.

'Nice! Sharp! Yeah, sweet, good speed.'

The knock came to the door. 'Five minutes, Decca!' Five minutes from a fight that would result in glory or failure. As I slipped into my St George tabard, my team formed around me to walk me down to the auditorium. The time had come. I had a job to do but still felt immense pressure to entertain the crowd and the punters that were watching on pay-per-view. I wanted people to remember this fight but, more than anything, I wanted to win. I had to win. This was my dream.

Julius was already in the ring, shuffling around and shadow-boxing, when my entrance music struck up: AC/DC's

'Thunderstruck' brought the crowd to their feet and ignited a frenzy of applause, cheers, jeers and whistling. As the first word of the lyrics rang out –'THUNDER' – I stepped into the spotlight. To the pounding rhythm and crackling guitar riffs of that heavy-metal anthem, I made my way to the ring. I didn't look at the crowd. I never do. I'm not there for them. I'm there to fight and they're there to see me fight. My eyes are fixed on the ring, to try to spot my opponent through the throng and the flag-waving ring-walkers. Easy in Julius's case – he was the biggest thing in that ring by far.

Ricky English made the introductions and, after due ceremony, the ring was cleared. Tabard removed, I turned and faced Julius across the ring. Fuck me! He is one enormous unit and, strangely enough, looked even bigger stripped off than he had when we'd met at The Blind Beggar for the signing of the contract. Fat, yeah! But in a fighter his size, that's just extra padding, and he had plenty. I had to get through all of that to have any chance of winding him, of hurting him, of putting him down. Body-shots played a big part of my preparation and soon I'd find out just how effective they'd be against his sizeable mass.

As I stepped into the ring and began to pace, Matt's advice was still ringing in my ears: 'Jab and step to his left to avoid his. Get over that leading arm and go for the side of his head with a big right.'

Sound enough tactics. Julius was reputed to have a left jab like a pile-driver.

'Hit him with those fast combos, followed by an upper-cut, and always shift to yer right as you come out or he'll catch you on the counter, yeah? And don't let him grab hold. He'll try an' lean on you to wear you down.'

I didn't speak; just listened. Yeah, yeah, got it: avoid clinches because, over six rounds, having a twenty-three stone colossus pushing down on you hastens fatigue. I slipped out of my tabard and made eye-contact with Matt as he checked my gloves. He gave me a knowing look. It said, 'This is it. You know what to do.'

'Seconds out!'

The crowd went crazy but I shut it out as we were called to the middle. We touched gloves, took a step back and then, from the bell, I went on the offensive. I'll be the first to admit this was not a classic fight but I'd challenge anyone who questioned my work rate. Six short rounds in a small ring favoured Julius, so I had to put in the graft. He could rely on his guile and ring-craft, stay fairly static and let me do all the work and that's exactly what he did. All his years of experience went into spoiling every attack.

The first round was typically cagey as we weighed each other up. I threw some good shots and he felt them but rode them, like the old pro he is. He'd retaliate with really accurate jabs that rarely missed their target. His easy-going, 'come and get me' routine was winding the punters up. I could hear a few jeers and people telling him to get stuck in, or calling him a lazy bastard. Lazy? *Nah!* Smart. He was up against a younger, fitter, lighter and more nimble fighter; a street-fighter, a bareknuckle bruiser. He wasn't being lazy, he was being canny. As for those who said he was past his prime? Trust me: that's not what it felt like on the receiving end.

Round two was more of the same, except I stepped up my work rate and pressed forward more. Julius just backed off and countered with that stiff, jarring left jab. Even sticking to Matt's game-plan, I couldn't get enough shots through his tight defence or over those massive arms and shoulders to land a telling blow. When I did, he'd just step back or grapple with me to stifle my combinations. In some of the clinches, I did manage to deliver some fierce upper-cuts but was a bit troubled by the fact that he was humming a tune the whole the time. Yes, you read it right: Julius was humming a tune to himself throughout the whole fight, between catching his breath whenever I got through and winded him with a fierce body-shot. Was this fucker on something?

Later he explained that it's a method he's always used to control his breathing and distract himself from the pain, and I was hurting him. In fact, I was never so proud as after the fight when he told Eamonn O'Keefe that he hadn't been hit that hard since he'd fought Mike Tyson. That's one quote I'll never forget – to be compared to one of my all-time fighting heroes, Michael Gerard Tyson (aka Kid Dynamite, aka Iron Mike, aka The Baddest Man on the Planet). I'll definitely take that as a compliment.

As expected, the fight rolled on, round after round of me on the offensive and Julius covering, blocking, spoiling and counter-punching. I like to think that the reason he adopted that tactic was that he'd underestimated me. Given what he said to Eamonn later, I'm fairly sure that my speed and power surprised him. You have to remember that I had barely had any boxing training before this fight and most bareknuckle bouts are short but vicious tear-ups. Fighting with gloves on was still alien to me and demands skills and disciplines I'm still only learning. Julius, on the other hand, was a veteran of forty-eight professional fights, many at the highest levels of the professional heavyweight division.

Maybe it was my inexperience but I even tried to gee him up

and whispered to him during a clinch something like, 'C'mon, Julius. Let's put on a show.' But he stuck to his game-plan of trying to control the pace by keeping it tight, covering up, spoiling, clinching and leaning on me or back against the ropes, waiting for an opening to land the big one.

My bid to become The Guv'nor had turned into a fuckin' siege. He was like an impregnable fortress under bombardment and, for all my pretty impressive firepower, I could not bring down those defences. Julius was obviously hoping that by the fifth or sixth round I'd run out of steam and he'd drop me with a hammer-blow. Wrong! I don't run out of steam and I kept pouring it on. But because I was having to take the fight to him, at times I was very exposed and Julius is too old a hand not to take advantage of those opportunities.

He caught me with a couple of real head-bangers, the biggest being in the third round. A massive left connected, which sent a shockwave right through my body that reached all the way down to my toes. I was in trouble and knew it but managed to keep my eyes focused on his to at least create the illusion I was OK. Had he realised I was momentarily stunned and totally helpless then followed through with a combination, I think he'd have dropped me but he didn't, thank Christ! I recovered my senses quickly enough to stumble sideways, as Matt had instructed, and fire off a right hook. Not one of my best shots, though enough to let him know that I was still in the game– but only just.

Saved by the bell, I slumped onto my stool, my head still spinning. Matt and Dean knew what they were looking at and immediately went to work, Dean fanning me with my towel, Matt forcing me to drink water, then splashing my face. He was hissing instructions and showing me the moves but I was still a bit groggy and not really taking it all in. All that mattered to me was that I had three rounds left to win that fight but wouldn't if I got caught by another clout like that.

You should have seen the bruises on my face the next day. I had one just above the temple, on the left side of my forehead, that was a couple of inches across. An inch lower and that shot might have been another that would have meant lights out; my lifelong dream destroyed and turned to a nightmare. I don't care what the armchair experts and social-media snipers say: Julius Francis may not be as mobile as he once was but he's lost none of his ring-craft and still has a counter-punch like a tank-buster.

Over the next three rounds, I waded in for all I was worth, hooking fiercely at his torso and switching to the head. Three rapid, *bang, bang, bang,* step right – *boom!* I must have done that over and over again but Julius just rolled out of every attack or dipped his head into his shoulder only for my knockout shot to glance off the top of his head. Other times he swatted away the head-shot or lunged and grappled my swinging arms to my sides. As I said, far from a classic but, fuck me, it was a hard day at the office from where I was standing. My fists thudded into his sides, upper arms and shoulders but he'd just grunt, hum some more and shift his stance. It was like pounding a one-tonne sack of wet sand. Knocking the fucker out was looking less and less likely.

The worst part of the fight for me was after the final bell. We were both still standing. The result was now out of my hands. Julius was blowing a little but looked good for another few rounds and I swear I could have gone another six. I felt I'd done more than enough but Teddy Bam-Bam had already raised Julius's arm and was parading him around the ring as the victor. My heart was wedged into my dry throat. Then Ricky English stepped through the ropes with the mic in his hand. Not for one moment in that fight had I been frightened but I was suddenly gripped by fear as he raised that mic to his lips to announce the winner.

'Ladies and gentlemen, the winner and new Guv'nor – Decca Heggie!

The crowd went wild. I caught my breath, then spun around to commiserate with Julius, who smiled and nodded as we patted each other on the back. The belt was presented and fastened around my waist and, with the mic now in my hand, I dedicated my victory to another Guv'nor – my hero: the late, great Lenny McLean. My impossible dream had become a reality.

I am the Guv'nor.

EPILOGUE

If you fight, you might lose. If you don't, you will never win. So whether your past is one of regret, pain and disappointment, or even one you're deeply ashamed of, just remember: tomorrow, the future – *your* future – is, as yet, unspoiled. Don't spoil tomorrow. Change today. Look forward, not back. Choose the future, not the past.

A very clever fella called Thomas Gray once wrote, 'The paths of glory lead but to the grave.'

Make a note of that, 'cause it's true. But it's down to you whether the path you carve through life leads to glory or mediocrity, or becomes a complete waste of a life *and*, being so precious, surely that is the greatest act of self-harm we can inflict upon ourselves. You have a limited time on this earth: don't abuse it – use it.

When the time comes, you're gonna want to look back down the path you carved and think, 'Well, I may have stumbled once or twice and deviated here and there occasionally but, you know what? Anyone who follows my path is gonna have few regrets when they finally reach the Pearly Gates – or return to the stars,' depending what your preferred scenario for the afterlife looks like.

Never stop exploring your potential and, when you find it, strive heart-and-soul to succeed. Do something with your life. Don't accept anything but the best from yourself and your path will be glorious. It doesn't have to lead to fame or fortune. Fame isn't all it's cracked up to be and, to use an old, worn out but no less true cliché, 'Money cannot buy you happiness.'

As your time draws to a close, the knowledge that you have loved and been loved will see you depart with the feeling that it has all been worthwhile. What more do any of us need in the end? Sorry, but I'm going to use another cliché: 'You can't take it with you.'

What you can take with you is the love and respect of others and you will have left your love secure in their hearts. But, hey! That's not a bad legacy for anyone to leave behind. Wouldn't you agree? So I recommend you start right now: show kindness, not cruelty; be pleased, not envious of others' successes, and invest heavily in love and happiness – they have a guaranteed return.

Oh, and remember: if you find that horrible Black Dog stalking you along the way, don't try and hide, 'cause the bugger'll dig you out. Turn and face it, defy it and don't be afraid to reach out for help – because help is out there.

Thank you for reading my story. Telling you about my life has helped me a lot and put a few things into perspective. I hope you, too, have gained something from it. Time alone will tell whether the next stage of my life will be worth writing about. I've got a feeling it might.

God bless – Decca.

IN MEMORIAM

Carl McVitie

22 January 1977–12 June 2016

Rest in peace, my friend.